THE McKINLEY AND ROOSEVELT
ADMINISTRATIONS

THE MACMILLAN COMPANY
NEW YORK · BOSTON · CHICAGO · DALLAS
ATLANTA · SAN FRANCISCO

MACMILLAN & CO., Limited
LONDON · BOMBAY · CALCUTTA
MELBOURNE

THE MACMILLAN CO. OF CANADA, Ltd.
TORONTO

THE
McKINLEY AND ROOSEVELT
ADMINISTRATIONS

1897–1909

BY

JAMES FORD RHODES, LL.D., D.LITT.

AUTHOR OF THE HISTORY OF THE UNITED STATES FROM THE
COMPROMISE OF 1850 TO THE FINAL RESTORATION OF HOME
RULE AT THE SOUTH IN 1877 ; HISTORICAL ESSAYS ;
LECTURES ON THE AMERICAN CIVIL WAR
DELIVERED AT OXFORD ; HISTORY
OF THE CIVIL WAR ; FROM
HAYES TO McKINLEY

New York
THE MACMILLAN COMPANY
1927

COPYRIGHT, 1922,

BY THE MACMILLAN COMPANY.

Set up and electrotyped. Published November, 1922.

Norwood Press
J. S. Cushing Co. — Berwick & Smith Co.
Norwood, Mass., U.S.A.

4037

CONTENTS

CHAPTER I

CHAPTER II

CHAPTER III

THE McKINLEY AND ROOSEVELT
ADMINISTRATIONS

THE McKINLEY AND ROOSEVELT ADMINISTRATIONS

1897–1909

CHAPTER I

THIS volume naturally begins with the political campaign of 1896 during which three men absorbed public attention — McKinley, Bryan and Marcus Alonzo Hanna, or, as he was familiarly called and will be known in this book, Mark Hanna. Of McKinley and Bryan, up to 1896, the student of affairs will have had some idea, but Mark Hanna deserves an introductory notice before the last eight years of his crowded life are related. Called an enigma in New York City, he was no enigma whatever to his intimates, except that they failed to gauge his towering ability. They knew him for a shrewd money-getter, able and diligent in business, but they could not believe that he would reach a high position in public affairs — that during one administration he would be known as the "king maker" and during another the champion of the financial magnates against Theodore Roosevelt — that he would at least divide with Roose-

1

velt the allegiance of the Labor Unions. In all essentials except political ability he was no enigma to his friends, for he wore his heart upon his sleeve.

New York City is a good point of survey and from this point Hanna's appearance in public life was like that of a comet in the sky. Although fifty-nine years old in 1896, he had gradually, but with steady ambition, been working up to the place from which he was now to begin his most important achievements. His restless mind had always cast about for a new enterprise and, not being a student or reader of books, and having no sympathy with a man who devoted his whole ability to the acquirement of money, he entered the field of politics. Before he was thirty-two he made an informal alliance with an enterprising young man of Cleveland to break up the Republican machine that dominated city politics. Both were good Republicans but objected to the manner in which city affairs were conducted. Somewhat later when the Republican machine nominated one of their representative men for mayor, Hanna led a revolt against the machine and, with the aid of a number of independent associates, nominated a Democrat of excellent business ability and elected him [1] although the rest of the Republican ticket was chosen. In city and ward politics, he was always noted for his independent action and often showed no hesitation in supporting Democrats when they were better men than the Republican nominees.

At the age of forty-three he was recognized as one of the prominent business men of Cleveland. His business was coal, iron ore and pig iron; in 1867 he had been started in it by his father-in-law, an iconoclast in society and

---

[1] In 1873.

trade and an uncompromising Democrat in politics. Hanna's independence however did not come from any family association; it was inherent in himself and gained for him the dislike of the solid financial men of Cleveland, who had built up the city and were naturally the dominant figures in its financial circles. In spite of the dislike of these magnates, Hanna pushed ahead until in 1880, the year of the Garfield campaign, he was known as a reliable Republican and had acquired a very considerable local prominence. He was head and front of the business men's meetings in Cleveland and fully favored making the campaign on the tariff and business issue rather than on the "bloody shirt." Closely connected with the Pennsylvania railroad through business relations, he formed a link between that great organization and the candidate of his party, afterwards president-elect. From that time on he never lost an opportunity to identify himself with any Republican movement. Although he had never read Cicero, he shared the Roman's belief that he must keep himself constantly before the public.

Hanna was attracted to the Civil Service Reform movement and attended the meeting of local organization in Cleveland.[1] He had no hope of being the president of the Cleveland association, but he did aspire to the chairmanship of the Executive Committee. The organization was controlled by men who did not like Hanna and who entirely ignored him in their dispositions, not even awarding him the consolation of membership on the Executive Committee, of which he would have liked to be the directing head. From that night, Hanna must have argued, there is a ring of reformers as well as a ring

---

[1] Either in January or February, 1882.

of politicians. I think the politicians will suit me
better.

His failure to secure election as district delegate to the
Republican National Convention of 1884 and his subsequent success in being chosen delegate at large gave him
an inkling of what was needed for political success. At
the Convention he was an avowed supporter of John
Sherman, whose candidacy met with little favor. He
opposed Blaine, yet when the Convention named him as
its candidate Hanna gained prominence in his party by
his earnest and sincere efforts for Blaine's election; but
no sooner was Blaine defeated than Hanna began to work
for Sherman's nomination in 1888. Securing the unanimous support of Ohio, a portion of Pennsylvania and
many delegates from the Southern States, he went to the
Convention as a delegate confident of success. In my
last volume I have told how Harrison's nomination came
to be made but, soon after Sherman's defeat, Hanna realized that under certain circumstances McKinley might
have been the man; accordingly he decided no longer
to put his money upon the wrong horse and became an
open advocate of McKinley's nomination for the next
presidency. Between 1890 and 1892 Hanna had serious
business troubles which, to a certain extent, distracted his
attention from politics and he was not as powerful a factor
in the Convention of 1892 as he had been four years before; he might have been thought to be losing his grip
on politics but he was simply biding his time. After the
astounding Republican victory in the election of 1894,
he went to his younger brother, then a business partner,
and told him that, for the future, he purposed giving more
time to politics and less to business. Arrangements were

made with this end in view and thenceforward he gave
nearly his entire attention to securing the nomination of
McKinley in 1896.

Boston, apart from a few men in State Street, did not
like Hanna. His brusque manner, unconventional talk,
ignorance of literature and art alienated many, and he
did not always live up to the moral ideals in politics that
were professed in this city. The general opinion was
afterwards well stated by Henry S. Pritchett, a true West-
erner, although at that time living in Boston, the efficient
President of the Massachusetts Institute of Technology.
"The papers to-day," he said in a speech to the Bowdoin
Alumni Association on February 16, 1904, "have been full
of the life of an interesting man, who now lies dead in
Washington. He was a strong man, a man of noble parts,
of splendid personal power and of high ability for service
and he has played a great part as a leader in this country.
He deserves for all that high praise. And yet we can
never forget in estimating him as a public man that he
must be judged, not only for his high personal qualities
but also for the quality of his public service. One cannot
fail to regret in looking back over that life that it should
have carried with it the noble qualities of devotion, of
energy, of ability and of loyalty to a friend and yet have
not had with it also a higher level of what public service
means . . . and a higher estimate of moral and intellectual force rather than pecuniary force in politics." [1]

New York City and other communities may have had
their opinions influenced by the prevalent caricatures
which always have something to do with the formation
of public sentiment. Hanna once said that, although

---

[1] Boston *Herald*, Feb. 17, 1904.

his ancestry was Scotch-Irish there was more Irish than Scotch in his composition; thus with a plausible exaggeration of his features he was often portrayed as a bloated whiskey-drinking Irishman. A much-repeated cartoon showed him and McKinley sitting over a bottle of whiskey in earnest confabulation. These caricatures caused his friends no little amusement, so entirely were they unfounded in fact. Hanna drank no wine until he was past middle life, did not care for it, and used stronger liquors only for medicinal purposes. McKinley preferred water to wine at a banquet or dinner or any other occasion. Indeed, if the cartoonist had shown McKinley and Hanna, sitting calmly together over a bottle of Waukesha or Poland water drinking to the toast "Here's to honest water which ne'er left man i' the mire," he would have been much nearer the truth.

"I shall never forget," said Senator Scott of West Virginia, "one morning during the campaign of 1896 when Hanna handed me a New York paper containing a cartoon of himself pictured as a huge monster, clad in a suit covered over with dollar marks, smoking an immense cigar, and trampling under foot women and children until their eyes protruded from the sockets and their skeleton forms writhed in agony. After I had looked at it for a moment he said to me, 'That hurts.' " [1]

This was a favorite caricature, Hanna covered all over with the dollar mark, the implication being that he believed money could buy anything. *The Nation* wrote during the heated political campaign of 1908: "The frankly commercial spirit in which Mark Hanna managed the two campaigns in which he was chairman is no-

[1] Address, April 7, 1904, 39.

torious. A prominent and honored Ohio Republican has said of Mr. Hanna that his only notion of political activity was 'to go out and buy somebody.' " [1] This remark, born probably of factional hostility, was unjust. Hanna paid the penalty of talking too frankly about the use of money,but no one knew better than he that money would not accomplish everything and, after he had gained power and influence, nothing perturbed him more than to be looked upon simply as an office-broker.

Collecting money for a political party must be regarded differently from getting means for the support of a church, a university or a charitable institution and, according to the cynical view of politics that obtains in certain quarters, the corruption of voters seems to inhere in the use of the party chest. But many voters looked upon the Republican party as something sacred, whose control was necessary to the well-being and perpetuity of the Republic. The man who raised money in order to insure its continuance in power was looked upon by them as doing holy work. Some such idea must have passed through Hanna's mind when, without concealment, he continually preached the use of money to save the party.

His outspoken scorn of bookish men and respect for those who had money to contribute lent color to *The Nation's* criticism, but in this matter and in others Hanna stood in need of a certain hypocrisy which was lacking in his nature. Making no bones of confessing his ignorance of Shelley and Pasteur, he loved Shakespeare as he saw his plays acted on the stage and took delight in a good performance of "School for Scandal," in Joseph Jefferson's "Rip Van Winkle," "Rivals" and "Cricket

---

[1] Oct. 8, p. 328.

on the Hearth." During the fifties when the Lyceum system was at its height, he was a constant attendant and liked above all the lectures of Ralph Waldo Emerson.

It is ordinarily thought that men in active life are apt to become victims of wine, woman or play. Judged by this standard, Hanna was a severely moral man who needed no refuge in the dictum of the preacher, "The moral man is he who is not found out." A generous giver of dinners, he was a spare eater except for an insatiable fondness for sweets to which his corpulence and rheumatism in later life were due. Loving the society of refined and well-bred women, he might be looked upon as a model of chastity. Passionately fond of cards, he preferred whist or bridge without a money stake; he never played draw poker except when a party for his favorite whist was unavailable and then only in what was known as a "small game." He had a pure mind, rarely told a smutty story and did not relish hearing one unless there was something in it that he thought clever. He was nevertheless rather undiscriminating in his response to humorous fancies and, though some of his intimates found in him an amusing companion, it was mainly his whole-hearted audacity that made them laugh. He gravitated toward the society of the best men. Amongst those one met at his dinner table in Washington were Root, Justice White, Taft, Long, O. H. Platt, Hobart, Allison, Aldrich and occasionally Secretary Hay and Senator Lodge.

Popular knowledge of a man of action who left few letters, did not keep a diary nor write a book depends largely upon his biographer and, in this respect, Hanna was exceptionally happy. His son selected Herbert Croly,

who made the work a labor of love and has presented the
real Mark Hanna with remarkable perspicacity and skill.
Some of Hanna's friends, on hearing of the selection, may
have shuddered at the thought of an author with social-
istic proclivities undertaking the biography of a strong
individualist; yet the accomplished editor of the American Statesmen series had chosen Carl Schurz, an avowed
tariff reformer, to write the life of Henry Clay and the
wisdom of this selection had been fully demonstrated.
Even so was the choice of Herbert Croly to write the life
of Mark Hanna.   One may learn from that book what
manner of man was Hanna when he determined to bend
all his energies to the nomination of McKinley in 1896.

Hanna and McKinley were warm personal friends.
They had first met in 1876 in the Court House at Canton,
Ohio, where were being tried one miner for assault with
intent to kill and a number of others for being engaged
in a riot.   Hanna as head of his Coal Company was active
in prosecution and McKinley was one of the attorneys
of the Stark County bar who had volunteered for the
defence.   It was a trial in which bitterness developed on
both sides and McKinley won attention from the prosecution by his personal resemblance to Daniel Webster,
and by his gentle consideration for the men who had
deemed it their duty to prosecute the offending miners.
In the same autumn McKinley was elected to Congress
and by degrees he and Hanna became intimate acquaintances.   At the National Convention of 1884, they shared
an apartment at a hotel; their relations were cordial
although McKinley was for Blaine and Hanna for Sherman.   The Convention of 1888, when they both supported
Sherman, increased the mutual attachment.   Each saw

qualities in the other that drew them together and, as both were working for the same end, they were now in complete sympathy.

Hanna's admiration for McKinley was profound. He shared his belief in the protective tariff as something sacred and not to be touched by profane hands. A man put forward for the presidential nomination should lose no opportunity of seeing influential men in the several States and commending himself to them by his personal bearing. Once when Hanna had with some difficulty secured an assemblage of men to meet the prospective candidate in an Eastern city, McKinley sent regrets on account of the illness of an invalid wife. This, for the moment, irritated Hanna as he thought that the wife might in her chronic condition have been left to the care of a doctor and nurse, as she was by no means dangerously ill and that McKinley might have kept the engagement which would have been a signal aid to his candidacy. This misfortune seemed to Hanna a considerable obstacle in the path of McKinley's advancement yet he was so struck with the man's sublime devotion to his invalid wife that he could not help exclaiming, "McKinley is a saint."

Hanna "had not a single small trait in his nature," declared Roosevelt. "I never needed to be in doubt as to whether he would carry through a fight or in any way go back on his word."[1]

Hanna's friendship with Ben Butterworth embodied a rare unselfishness that dignified his strenuous and successful career. Croly prints some letters from Butterworth to Hanna that are charming in the devotion shown by

---

[1] Croly, 361.

him who stuck to the lesser man through thick and thin.
Butterworth was of too independent and impulsive a
nature to be successful in politics but his honest appearance and conduct gave him a standing with leaders that
he seemed unable to acquire with the mass. When he
was unsuccessful in politics Hanna redoubled his assistance and when at last he fell fatally ill Hanna watched by
his bedside in a Cleveland hotel with the same devotion
that he would pay to a brother.

The campaign for the nomination was proceeding apace
when McKinley gave it a set-back through his own financial failure. He made himself liable by endorsements to
help a friend for one hundred and thirty thousand dollars,
a large sum in 1893 and an enormous one for the Governor of Ohio. He had no other idea than that the debt
must be paid in full and it seemed to him as if the labor
necessary to this end meant the close of his political career.
But Hanna, Myron T. Herrick, H. H. Kohlsaat and many
others came to his aid and saved him from bankruptcy.
These facts were more or less publicly known and
McKinley was reproached with having put himself in
the power of these men by accepting financial favors for
which they would expect repayment in some way. But it
does not appear that any of them asked for consideration
nor that anything was done for the raisers of the fund
except for Hanna and Herrick who received McKinley's
support on entirely different grounds.[1]

---

[1] In this characterization I have been helped by Life of Hanna, Herbert
Croly; Mark Hanna, Solon Lauer, Cleveland, 1901; William Allen White's
article, *McClure's Magazine*, Nov. 1900; Murat Halstead, *Review of
Reviews*, Oct. 1896; the contemporary cartoons; many newspaper notices
of Hanna's death in Feb. 1904. My son, Daniel P. Rhodes, was private
secretary of Mark Hanna for a year and a half covering 1897 and a part
of 1898; to him I owe a careful revision of this whole chapter.

Croly has related in sufficient detail Hanna's labor in securing the nomination of McKinley. From January 1, 1895, his whole attention was devoted to the work and everything that energy, social entertainment, political blandishment and the judicious use of money could accomplish was forthcoming in full measure. He spent, said Croly, "something over $100,000" (which would not now [1] be considered a large amount) obtaining almost no assistance from his friends. "Corrupt methods were always expressly and absolutely forbidden," wrote Croly, but when Hanna put in his own time and energy he could make a dollar go a great way, as he did in this case although he had opposed to him Quay and Thomas C. Platt, adepts in all the arts of political management, as well as a hearty New England backing of Thomas B. Reed who, by common consent, was well fitted for the place. Yet it was not Hanna's work alone that won the prize. McKinley, in capacity and manner, was well fitted for the White House; moreover, since 1893, affairs had been working his way. The panic of 1893 had been followed by a commercial crisis and business was extremely bad. The Republicans ascribed the evil condition to Democratic success and to the avowed promise of a reduction of the tariff. The tariff was reduced during the summer of 1894 and the autumn elections for Congressmen showed a complete change in public sentiment. It was natural that a distracted public should turn to the arch-protectionist for relief. McKinley was reëlected Governor of Ohio in 1893 by an increased majority [2] and in geographical and all other respects was an available candidate.

---

[1] 1919.   [2] For McKinley's first election see my vol. viii. 374.

Henry Clay said in the bitterness of his disappointment at failing to receive the Whig nomination in 1840,
"If there were two Henry Clays, one of them would make
the other President of the United States." [1]   But
McKinley's and Hanna's relations were so intimate that
Hanna might be called an alter-ego. What one could
not do, the other could. McKinley knew the men in
public life through and through, and Hanna learned how
to manipulate conventions and secure delegates; and he
thought that he was serving party and country well in
putting to the fore an arch-protectionist. By May 1,
1896, if not before, Hanna felt that McKinley's nomination was assured, but before the Convention met on
June 16 in St. Louis the question of platform was the
most important one, and the only portion on which there
was a marked divergence of opinion related to silver;
this difference grew as the time for the assembling of the
Convention approached. When the delegates began to
come together, the Committee on Resolutions, of which
Foraker was the chairman and Senator Lodge the Massachusetts member, had many declarations to consider but,
out of the confusion and heat of convention days, only
two resolutions are important for the historian; these
are the McKinley-Hanna resolution, which Hanna brought
with him to Chicago, and the resolution finally adopted
by the Convention, on which the canvass of 1896 was
made.

Both McKinley and Hanna were bimetallists. While
in Congress, McKinley had in 1877 and 1878 voted for
free silver, for the Bland-Allison bill and for its passage
over President Hayes's veto; but in his support of silver

---

[1] Schurz's Clay, ii. 181.

he was backed by both senators from Ohio and all the representatives except James A. Garfield. In the discussions of Garfield's course, which were of daily occurrence among business men in Cleveland, his dissenting voice was generally approved, but Hanna vigorously opposed his position and endorsed that of the other members, especially of the representative from Cleveland, who was a personal and political friend. Thus McKinley and Hanna had been favorable to silver for eighteen years when it fell to them to decide the issue on which the campaign of 1896 should be made. And they both, for obvious reasons to anyone who understands their political careers, desired to have the paramount issue the tariff, while silver should be relegated to a subsidiary place.

In 1896 in Ohio it was no disgrace to be a bimetallist. It was much easier to favor a single gold standard in New York or Boston; yet in Boston some of the most eminent statesmen, authors, business men and politicians, under the brilliant leadership of General Walker, had embraced the doctrine of silver and, though opposing the free coinage of the metal, were eager for its adoption as a money standard by international agreement. Between 1894 and 1896 many of these Bostonians were converted to a single gold standard although they still held to the fiction of international agreement which, as the wisest of them knew, was out of the question. This conversion was undoubtedly due to the great work of Grover Cleveland and while most Republicans would have spurned the idea of having been so influenced yet to the historian it appears that they were thus unconsciously swayed.

In the pre-Convention days in St. Louis the Eastern

men, whose leader may be said to have been Senator
Lodge, were eager for the mention of gold; many from
the Middle West desired a plank which could be inter-
preted as favoring gold in the East and yet not condemn-
ing silver in the West. The McKinley-Hanna resolution read: The Republican party "would welcome
bimetallism based upon an international ratio, but, until
that can be secured, it is the plain duty of the United
States to maintain our present standard, and we are therefore opposed under existing conditions to the free and
unlimited coinage of silver at sixteen to one." Before
these words, it spoke of "maintaining all the money of
the United States whether gold, silver or paper at par
with the best money in the world and up to the standard
of the most enlightened governments." The resolution
adopted by the Convention, which was agreed to by Senator Lodge and his associates, read: "We are opposed
to the free coinage of silver except by international agreement with the leading commercial nations of the world,
which we pledge ourselves to promote, and until such
agreement can be obtained the existing *gold* standard
must be preserved. All our silver and paper currency
must be maintained at parity with gold and we favor all
measures designed to maintain inviolably the obligations
of the United States and all our money, whether coin or
paper at the present standard, the standard of the most
enlightened nations of the earth." It is easy to see that
the controversy turned on a few words. Should the Republican party "maintain our present standard" or preserve "the existing *gold* standard"? To the historian
conversant with the action of Grover Cleveland, the difference does not seem great, but to the framer of platforms

and the campaigner it was immense. One resolution
declared in favor of gold by name, the other did not;
hence it turned out that the Republicans were known
throughout the campaign as the party of gold, the Democrats as the party of silver. It is no wonder, then, that
the adoption of this resolution is considered so important
an episode in the history of the Republican party and of
the country, and that so many lay claim to a paramount
influence in securing its insertion.

When Hanna saw that, owing to the sentiment developed among the delegates, his own view could not prevail, he accepted the result gracefully and persuaded
McKinley to do likewise. The Committee agreed on the
financial plank and reported it to the Convention, which
adopted it by a vote of 812½ to 110½. Before the adoption of this plank, Senator Teller of Colorado offered a substitute demanding the free coinage of silver but obtained
only 105½ votes against 818½; this vote foreshadowed
the adoption of the financial plank by nearly the same
majority. After making some pathetic remarks, he,
with thirty-three others, seceded from the Convention.
The rest of the platform was then adopted by acclama-
tion.[1]

McKinley was then nominated by 661½ votes, his leading opponent, Thomas B. Reed, receiving 84½. Garret
A. Hobart of New Jersey was named for Vice President.

---

[1] Life of Hanna, Croly; Foraker, Notes of a Busy Life, i.; Charles
Emory Smith, *Philadelphia Press*, June 24, 1896, cited by *Boston Daily
Advertiser;* The Autobiography of T. C. Platt; MS. statement of Eben
S. Draper, Chairman of the Mass. delegation, Jan. 9, 1900; H. H. Kohlsaat's story, *N. Y. Eve. Post*, April 30, 1910; Letter of Frank S. Wither-
bee, *N. Y. Eve. Post*, April 13, 1910; W. A. White, *McClure's*, Nov.
1900; Halstead in *Review of Reviews*, Oct. 1896; Lodge, Speeches
and Addresses, 1900; Stanwood, Hist. of the Presidency.

On June 18 when McKinley was nominated, Republican success was deemed more than probable. Mark Hanna was made Chairman of the Republican National Committee but thought of taking a yacht cruise along the New England Coast to obtain a needed rest after "the great strain" imposed by the work resulting in McKinley's nomination. "I would have been glad," he wrote in a private letter, "to have escaped the responsibility of managing the campaign, but there was no way out of it and I feel that I am 'enlisted for the war' and *must* win." This letter was written on July 3 when Hanna had no idea that he had an easy victory before him; as between June 18 and July 3 public sentiment showed that the Republican party in identifying itself with gold had run the risk of losing some of the Western States. "I must get the work of education started," he said, "before I can take my necessary recreation." "The fight will be in the Mississippi Valley States," he added. "The 'gold' basis is giving us lots of work." [1]

The Democratic Convention in Chicago, meeting on July 7, defined the issue plainly between gold and silver and changed the hoped-for victory of the Republicans into a premonition of defeat. There were many indications that the Democrats would espouse the cause of free silver. Richard P. Bland of Missouri was their idol, leader and probable candidate for the presidency and he had publicly said that the Democracy of the West was convinced that "the gold standard meant bankruptcy" and that the Convention would declare for the "free coinage of silver at 16 to 1." [2] The delegates who were

---

[1] Letter from Cleveland.
[2] Twenty Years of the Republic, Peck, 492.

known as Cleveland men made a valiant fight, but their financial plank was rejected by 303 to 626 and their endorsement of Cleveland's administration by 357 : 564. During the discussion of the financial resolution, William J. Bryan leaped into prominence through a speech that carried the Convention. "Upon which side will the Democratic party fight," he asked, "upon the side of the idle holders of idle capital or upon the side of the struggling masses? . . . Having behind us the producing masses of this nation and the world, supported by the commercial interests, the laboring interests and the toilers everywhere, we will answer their demand for a gold standard by saying to them : 'You shall not press down upon the brow of labor this crown of thorns, you shall not crucify mankind upon a cross of gold.' " [1] The platform as reported by the Committee on Resolutions was adopted by 628 to 301. It declared that, "Gold monometallism is a British policy and its adoption has brought other nations into financial servitude to London. . . . We demand the free and unlimited coinage of both silver and gold at the present legal ratio of sixteen to one without waiting for the aid or consent of any other nation." [2] Some of the other resolutions were judged to be "anarchistic"; they were certainly extremely radical for 1896.

Bryan's speech, especially the last clause of the last sentence cited above, made him the Democratic candidate for the presidency.

"The Chicago convention has changed everything," wrote Hanna in a private letter on July 16. It has knocked out my holiday and cruise along the New England coast. The campaign "will be work and hard work

---

[1] Bryan, The First Battle, 206.   [2] Stanwood, 542.

from the start.   I consider the situation in the West quite
alarming as business is all going to pieces and idle men
will multiply rapidly. With this communistic spirit
abroad the cry of 'free silver' will be catching."   Both
Hanna and McKinley felt that the Republican party was
united on the tariff but divided on the silver question.
During a conference, probably before Bryan's nomination, McKinley said, "I am a Tariff man standing on a
Tariff platform. This money matter is unduly prominent. In thirty days you won't hear anything about
it," when William R. Day [1] remarked, "In my opinion in
thirty days you won't hear of anything else." [2]   Even
after the Chicago Convention, Hanna expressed himself
as not wishing to allow the tariff issue to be over-
shadowed by the financial.[3] But the logic of events
taught both McKinley and Hanna that a determined
fight must be put up against free silver in the Western
States; and in point of fact their belief in bimetallism,
but only on an international basis, proved as effective in
the conduct of the campaign as if they had been uncompromising advocates of the single gold standard.

The Republican secession affected the vote in some of
the Western States but the Democratic "bolt" was more
significant. It took two forms: one, the nomination of
separate candidates for President and Vice President
known as gold Democrats, and the other votes given directly to McKinley as the surest means of beating Bryan.

There is no question that business was much depressed
and that many men were out of employment. The Republicans had hoped to charge this condition to the Dem-

---

[1] Now Justice of the United States Supreme Court (1919).
[2] Life of McKinley, Olcott, 321.   [3] Life of Foraker, i. 492.

ocratic administration and to the Tariff bill of 1894, and therefore McKinley, who represented protection more than any other man in the country, was the logical candidate. He was the "advance agent of prosperity" and promised the "full dinner pail"; prosperity was to be secured by a return to the protective tariff of the Republican party. On the other hand, the Bryan Democrats, though agreeing to the Republican estimate of present conditions, promised an entirely different remedy for the hard times, and proposed a different policy for reducing the army of the unemployed. Remonetize silver, coin it at the ratio of 16 to 1, stop measuring money by the English standard but increase its volume, they averred, and the distress of men in legitimate business and of honest laborers out of employment will disappear. The demonetization of silver enhanced the value of the circulating medium and was in the interest of the creditor; restore it to its proper place, they argued, and the augmented circulation will enable the debtor to pay his debts and start all the wheels of industry going.

Bryan proved an effective campaigner, although his first move was not successful. Determined to open the campaign in "the enemy's country" he formally accepted the nomination in a speech in Madison Square Garden, New York City. But he committed an error in reading the speech which he had carefully written out. For Bryan, though an orator, was a poor reader. Other conditions were against him. The weather, even for the second week of August, was extremely hot and the notification speech unduly long. The large audience who had expected to laugh at "his free Western sallies and audacities" found him "transformed into a Professor

Dryasdust prosing through two mortal hours. . . . No wonder that they fled before his portentous pile of manuscript with cries of 'Good-night, Billy.'" [1]

New York and other Eastern financial centres breathed a sigh of relief. They had been greatly alarmed at Bryan's stirring speech before his nomination and his short addresses on the way from Lincoln to New York City, but now they heard or read a dull economic argument, which could not carry conviction to thinking men and which utterly failed to rouse the proletariat. Depression at the fear that Bryan and his financial fallacies would carry the country was succeeded by a momentary and undue elation of the conservative forces.

But when Bryan began his trip through the country, his native ability as an orator and his sincere belief in the fallacies that he advocated gained him large audiences and shaped convictions. Farmers, obliged to accept a low price for their products, and laborers, who desired work but could not get it, were glad to learn that free silver was the one simple remedy for their trouble. The distress was indeed grave. If we subtract from Dr. Talmage's remarks what they contained of rhetorical exaggeration, an extract from his non-partisan sermon will give us an excellent idea. "Never within my memory," he said, "have so many people literally starved to death as in the past few months. Have you noticed in the newspapers how many men and women here and there have been found dead, the post-mortem examination stating that the cause of death was hunger? There is not a day when we do not hear the crash of some great

---

[1] *The Nation*, Aug. 20, 134.

commercial establishment and as a consequence many people are thrown out of employment. Among what we considered comfortable homes have come privation and close calculation and an economy that kills. Millions of people who say nothing about it are at this moment at their wits' end. There are millions of people who do not want charity but want work." [1]

Goldwin Smith, a keen observer, felt Bryan's "preternatural power of clap-trap declamation." [2] The Democratic National Committee coöperated skilfully with their candidate and made their appeal for funds in an attractive manner. Their pressing need was the hiring of speakers and the distribution of documents "for the dissemination of the truth." One hundred and twenty-five thousand of "Coin's Financial School" were circulated, a device that showed how clever they were. This little book was made up of addresses purporting to be delivered daily to large Chicago audiences, that were hereby instructed in the science of money by Coin, a "smooth little financier." The fascination of his manner, his ready argument, apparent fairness, cannot fail to charm even the reader of to-day who knows that the school was a fiction designed to serve as the subject of an attractive book in which fallacious arguments might be presented that would otherwise remain unheard. So this amiable-looking little man was supposed to deliver six lectures from the platform of a large hall of the Art Institute; and these were attended fictitiously by men prominent in business and finance, who were argued with and either convinced or refuted. This was not a difficult

---

[1] Sept. 27. The First Battle, Bryan, 474.
[2] *Sat. Rev.*, Oct. 31, 462.

mitting, for the moment, that Iowa must be placed in the doubtful column, he was still confident of McKinley's election, believing that at the worst it would be a close shave, while he really hoped for a stampede. At any rate, the campaign was to him too serious a matter for any phase of it to be left to chance; indeed, he and McKinley had decided that, if matters got desperate, McKinley should take the stump in Illinois, Indiana, Michigan, Iowa and Kansas.

The Methodist, the Roman Catholic and the other churches were mainly on the side of sound money and many preachers did not hesitate to bring politics into the pulpit during their Sunday exhortations. Nature gave a welcome help to Hanna in an advance in the price of wheat. Now do something for corn came a witty demand from the Indian corn-growing States.

To Bryan's oratory more than to any other one cause was due the impression that the campaign was one of the masses against the classes. Some of the resolutions of the Chicago platform were deemed anarchistic [1] and influenced votes against Bryan who thought it wise to deny the imputation. "We have been called anarchists," he said. "I am not an anarchist. There is not beneath the flag a truer friend of government or a greater lover of law and order than the nominee of the Chicago convention." [2] It is difficult to describe with strict impartiality a heated political campaign in one's own country and one's own time, but a keen observer from England should have been able to view the events of 1896 with a comparative lack of bias. "I have never thought the Republic in [such] serious peril as I do now," wrote Gold-

---

[1] *Ante.*   [2] Speech in Baltimore during September, 463.

win Smith, "when I see the organization of the Democratic party captured by Anarchism and Repudiation. Bimetallism, you will understand, is the least part of the matter; even Repudiation is not the greatest. The greatest is the uprising of disorder, in all its forms and grades against the institutions of the American Republic. . . . Bryanism is a vast cave of Adullam, in which are combined all the distressed, all the discontented, all who have nothing to lose and may hope to gain by a general overturn. . . . In November the Republic of the Fathers will be fighting for its life." [1]

During October the stampede to McKinley took place. General J. D. Cox, who was then living in Cincinnati, Ohio, wrote on October 26 in a private letter: "When I went East in June I am sure nine-tenths of the Ohio Republicans were ardent bimetallists, with more leaning to free silver than to gold monometallism. Now nearly every man seems to rival his neighbor in putting gold forward as the single standard. . . . The claim of Republican managers that there is a 'landslide' going on in McKinley's favor, I assume to be sufficiently true to warrant a confident expectation of his election."

Bryan made a wonderful canvass, travelling 18,000 miles and addressing audiences almost every day. The mere fact of his bearing the physical strain he was undergoing and the eagerness of people to see and hear this famous orator must have counted in his favor.[2]

---

[1] *Saturday Review*, Aug. 1, Sept. 5, Oct. 31.

[2] In this account of the campaign of 1896, I have been assisted by Croly's Life of Hanna; Olcott's Life of McKinley; Bryan, The First Battle; Peck; Stanwood, Hist. of the Presidency; *The Nation, passim;* Goldwin Smith's articles in the *Saturday Review;* Foraker, Notes of a Busy Life, i.; Conversations with Mark Hanna, Aug. 23, Dec. 20.

On Tuesday, November 3, nearly fourteen millions voted. McKinley was triumphantly elected. He was to receive 271 electoral votes to Bryan's 176, a majority of 95. His plurality in the popular vote was somewhat over six hundred thousand. "No President since U. S. Grant," wrote Croly, "entered office supported by so large a proportion of the American people as did William McKinley." [1] Bryan congratulated McKinley on his election and the successful candidate made a graceful reply.

McKinley carried the New England States, New York, New Jersey and Pennsylvania by large majorities. The Middle Western States gave him their electoral votes. He invaded the solid South, carrying Delaware, Kentucky, West Virginia and Maryland, Maryland by an imposing plurality. Bryan carried Kansas and Nebraska, all the mining States except California, and also Washington, while Oregon voted for McKinley. North Dakota did likewise, while South Dakota gave her electoral vote to Bryan by a small plurality. Ohio, the State of McKinley and Hanna, was a disappointment to the Republicans. While they never regarded seriously the boasts of the Bryanites that they would carry the State, yet her plurality, being less than that of Michigan and about one third that of Illinois, showed that Ohio was somewhat uncertain. For, in the August forecast, Michigan was set down as very doubtful and, while Illinois was considered less doubtful, she was not regarded, like Ohio, as safe beyond peradventure for McKinley.

---

[1] P. 227.

CHAPTER II

AFTER the election of McKinley, Mark Hanna occupied an enviable position. Had it been usual, the freedom of Cleveland would have been conferred upon him. "He can own this city," said an enthusiastic financial adherent. "What a glorious record Mark Hanna has made this year!" wrote John Hay in a private letter. "I never knew him intimately until we went into this fight together, but my esteem and admiration for him have grown every hour. He is a born general in politics, perfectly square, honest and courageous with a *coup d'œil* for the battle-field, and a knowledge of the enemy's weak points which is very remarkable. I do not know whether he will take a share in the government, but I hope he will." [1] McKinley desired him to accept a Cabinet position and for a while he revolved in his mind whether he would not take the post of Secretary of the Treasury, a place which he was entitled to and which he would have admirably filled. On looking into the matter, however, he found the routine and confinement of the office objectionable; moreover, he aspired after the senatorship from his State — an office that would give him the influence he desired to exert, and yet effectually preserve his independence. Therefore he made public the declaration that he would accept no office from the McKinley administration.

---

[1] Croly, 228.

Hanna did not appreciate that this statement would rise up to plague him. For he had conceived the idea of inducing the President to appoint Senator John Sherman Secretary of State and of being appointed by the Governor of Ohio to succeed him for his unexpired term in the Senate [March 4, 1899]. During his many interviews and conferences with McKinley he canvassed the matter, with the result that on January 4, 1897, the President-elect offered to Sherman the position of Secretary of State in his administration, and this was promptly accepted.[1] The course of events gave efficient support to those who wished to attack McKinley and Hanna, as it demonstrated that the appointment was utterly unfit owing to mental failure on the part of the Secretary of State. The critics averred that Sherman had given way to unusual excitement, both on the floor of the Senate and in a newspaper interview, that his memory had been failing for two or three years, that this fact was so presented to Hanna and McKinley that they ought to have recognized it, staying their hands from such procedure ; that it was in short, a case of an aged statesman being "kicked upstairs" to make a place for Mark Hanna. Sherman himself, after the resignation of the office of Secretary of State [April 25, 1898] by newspaper interview and private letter, confirmed this criticism. "No doubt," he wrote confidentially on November 8, 1898, "I ought to have remained in the Senate during my term, which would not have expired until the 4th of March next. At that time I regarded McKinley as a sincere and ardent friend, whom I had assisted and whose election I had promoted. When

---

[1] Life of McKinley, Olcott, 329.

he urged me to accept the position of Secretary of State, I accepted with some reluctance and largely to promote the wishes of Mark Hanna. The result was that I lost the position both of Senator and Secretary. . . . They deprived me of the high office of Senator by the temporary appointment as Secretary of State." [1]

Wisdom after the event is the source of much criticism, and so it is in this case when the well-meant plan of Hanna and McKinley turned out badly. Hanna had twice supported Sherman for the presidential nomination, and had a high idea of his wisdom, not only in finance but in foreign affairs; seeing something of his work as chairman of the Committee on Foreign Relations in the Senate, he admired his clear comprehension and effective statement, and as he felt in a measure responsible for the success of the McKinley administration, he really thought that he was contributing to it by helping Sherman to the leading place in the Cabinet. His attitude to the stories that came to him regarding Sherman's mental failure was characteristic; he had such confidence in Sherman's ability and so desired the succession to the Senate that he did not believe the stories, even though some of them must have been endorsed by his New York financial friends to whom he had been drawn closely by the exigencies of the political campaign. He knew Sherman well socially; was aware that he had always been temperate in eating and drinking, moderate in all of his pleasures and, although nearly 74, could not see that there

---

[1] Notes of a Busy Life, Foraker, i. 508. Sherman died in 1900. This letter was handed to Foraker by General Miles, March 1, 1902, but was not printed until the first edition of this book, which was published in February, 1916.

was any reason for thinking, apart from the stories that were afloat, that he might not be physically and mentally fit for six years to come. *The Nation,* which became a severe critic of the appointment, said in an editorial on August 20, 1896: "Senator Sherman can make a good speech when he tries to do so. His speech at Columbus on Saturday was one of the best he has ever made." [1]

McKinley's first impression against Sherman's appointment was entirely different from the result. The Senator was generally considered as the leader of his party in his State and McKinley feared that on account of his masterfulness he would wish to dominate the administration. It is not surprising, therefore, that with this idea fixed in his mind McKinley should have made little account of the reports that he heard of Sherman's mental failure and should write to Joseph Medill on February 8, 1897: "I concur in your opinion that the stories regarding Senator Sherman's 'mental decay' are without foundation and the cheap inventions of sensational writers or other evil-disposed or mistaken people. When I saw him last [this was January 15, 1897] I was convinced both of his perfect health physically and mentally, and that his prospects of life were remarkably good." [2]

Sherman was glad to accept the Secretaryship of State. He exchanged two years in the Senate with a doubtful succession for apparently a four years' tenure of the Cabinet head of the new Republican administration, which was undoubtedly a promotion. It was not unusual, however, for Senators to decline Cabinet appoint-

---

[1] P. 134; see also June 24, 1897.
[2] Life of McKinley, Olcott, i. 334.

ments, and it was open to Sherman to do so, but as matter of fact the prospect was attractive. He had enjoyed himself in the Treasury Department under Hayes, having great influence with the President and he might well have thought that a similar experience now awaited him.

The important question was, would Governor Asa Bushnell appoint Hanna? The two belonged to different factions in the Republican party in Ohio and there was no love lost between them. Sherman used his influence to get the Governor to name Hanna as his successor, and the President-elect wrought powerfully in his friend's behalf. Nevertheless the Governor did not want to appoint a factional enemy and he authorized his personal and political friend, Joseph B. Foraker, to offer the place to Theodore E. Burton of Cleveland, then a Representative in Congress who, however, declined it. During the first part of February, McKinley must have despaired of the carrying out of this part of the program, as he still urged Hanna to accept a Cabinet position, writing to him on February 18, 1897, "I have hoped, and so stated to you at every convenient opportunity, that you would yet conclude to accept the Postmaster-Generalship." The Treasury was no longer at the President-elect's disposal, as on January 28 he had authorized the announcement that he had selected for that post Lyman J. Gage of Chicago.[1] "You have as often declined," McKinley continued in this letter to Hanna, "and since our conversation on Tuesday last (February 16) I have reluctantly concluded that I cannot induce you to take this or any other

---

[1] *The Nation*, Feb. 4.

Cabinet position. You know how deeply I regret this determination and how highly I appreciate your life-long devotion to me. You have said that if you could not enter the Senate you would not enter public life at all."

Those who like to consider the "might have been" may conjecture whether, if Hanna had even now decided to go into the Cabinet, McKinley would have induced Sherman to withdraw his acceptance of the office of Secretary of State on the ground that he would prefer not to have two men from Ohio in his Cabinet? In which event he would have appointed as Secretary of State a man flatly opposed to a warlike intervention in favor of Cuba, as at that time McKinley was himself.

Hanna, more persistent than McKinley, had no idea of giving up the game. Bushnell was a candidate for the Republican nomination for Governor who would be elected in the autumn of 1897, and, if he failed to appoint Hanna Senator, he would jeopardize materially his chance of nomination. Finally, through fear of failing to receive the renomination he desired, and from the unmistakable sentiment in the Republican party in Ohio that Hanna should have the place, he determined to appoint his ancient enemy, and wrote to him on February 21, "I wish to communicate to you my conclusion to appoint you as the successor of Senator Sherman when his resignation shall have been received." [1]

William McKinley was inaugurated on March 4, 1897, and in his address made clear the immediate policy of the

---

[1] Life of Hanna, Croly, 240. This book has been used freely in this account. Also Foraker, Notes of a Busy Life, i.; Life of McKinley, Olcott; John Sherman, Theodore E. Burton; do. W. S. Kerr, ii.; *The Nation, passim.*

government.[1]   There were "depression in business, distress among the people."   The government needed more
revenue and ought to get it by an increase in tariff
taxation.   On this point he spoke to a united party
and had Congress and Republicans with him; to carry
out this purpose he summoned an extra session for
March 15.

The position which McKinley took need not have surprised anyone; nevertheless, the gold Democrats who had
supported him were disappointed that he did not put the
money question to the fore and advocate legislation
which should fix by law permanently the gold standard;
this development received fit expression in the speeches
of ex-President Cleveland and ex-Secretary Carlisle at the
New York City Reform Club dinner of April 24.   Cleveland could speak with authority, as he was the hero of
the gold standard even as McKinley was the apotheosis of
a protective tariff.   And Cleveland and his Cabinet had
given McKinley a hearty welcome, unusual in a change of
one party administration to its opponent.   But McKinley was wiser than his critics in declaring that the securing
of adequate revenue must precede financial legislation.
So far as finance was concerned he must endeavor to effect
international bimetallism; until that was decided, the existing gold standard would be maintained.   The President knew that no act such as he desired could pass the
existing Senate, and his foresight was confirmed by that
body adopting, within less than a year, a resolution which
declared that the principal and interest of the government bonds were payable in silver dollars at the option

[1] The Inaugural Address is printed in Cong. Record, xxx. Pt. 1.   For
McKinley's Cabinet, see Peck, 521.

of the administration.[1] McKinley made a sincere attempt to obtain international bimetallism but, when Great Britain blocked the way,[2] he appreciated that business in the United States must be conducted on the single gold standard. In the attempt to secure this by proper legislation, he said, in a confidential talk with Senator Hanna and Secretary Alger on one of the last evenings of August, 1897, the Republican party may go down and I may go down with it but, after that temporary sacrifice, the Republican party devoted to such a noble cause will rise again.

Everything was in proper shape to enact a protective tariff to take the place of the Democratic Act of 1894. It had been tacitly agreed that Thomas B. Reed should be reëlected Speaker of the new House, and Nelson Dingley, also of Maine, should be chairman of the Committee on Ways and Means; this tacit agreement was at once carried into effect. This Committee, which was substantially the same as that of the preceding Congress, had at that session, after hearing abundant testimony, prepared a tariff bill which was now introduced into the House and passed on March 31. The Senate offered many amendments and did not pass their bill until July 7, when it went to a Committee of conference whose report was adopted by the House on July 19 by yeas 187, nays 116, and by the Senate on July 24 by yeas 40, nays 30 ; on this day the President signed it and it became a law.

"We expect," Dingley had written in a private letter, "to cut nearly all our duties considerably below those of

---

[1] Life of McKinley, Olcott, i. 358. It was a concurrent resolution. It passed the Senate by a vote of 47 : 32 on Jan. 28, 1898, and was rejected by the House on Jan. 31, the vote standing 133 : 181.   [2] Ibid., 355.

the Act of 1890." [1] To no better man could the tariff bill have been confided. No one in public life, except McKinley and Senator Aldrich, understood the subject better. For Dingley, it was a labor of love, and with the assistance especially of Sereno E. Payne of New York and John Dalzell of Pennsylvania, fellow members of the Committee, he presented to the House "a fairly good protectionist measure." [2] As showing the confidence felt in him by the President, he had been offered the Treasury Department which, on account of a question of health, he had declined, but saying at the same time that he could do more for the success of the administration as chairman of the Committee on Ways and Means than he could in the Treasury.[3] The measure is quite properly called the Dingley Act and is so known in history.

When Nelson W. Aldrich of Rhode Island reported the bill from the Senate Committee on Finance, he said that it was "thoroughly understood throughout the country in the last political campaign, that if the Republican party should be again entrusted with power, no extreme tariff legislation would follow." [4] Dingley and Aldrich expressed the idea of the Republican leaders and, while the House was readily controlled by the power of the Speaker Thomas B. Reed, it was quite different when the tariff question was opened up in the Senate. It was as John Sherman had previously said, "When Republicans and Democrats together are framing a tariff, each Member or Senator consults the interest of his 'district' or State." [5]

---

[1] Tarbell, Tariff in Our Time, 242.   [2] Ibid., 243.
[3] Life and Times of Nelson Dingley, 413.
[4] Stanwood, American Tariff Controversies, ii. 384.
[5] Recollections, ii. 1085.

Copyright by Courtney.

William McKinley

A feature of the case in hand is told by Edward Stanwood, "The plans of the Republican leaders were overturned . . . by senators who were more in favor of silver than of a protective tariff." [1]   The Dingley Act, when it became a law, had rates of duty higher than they had been under any preceding tariff.[2]   The McKinley Act was a 49½ per cent tariff, the Wilson, 40 to 41¾, while the percentage of the Dingley Act ran from 49⅞ to 52.[3]

McKinley enjoyed the first few months of his presidential life more than the later ones. As he did the honors of the White House, he appeared to have lived there always, so well did he fit into the place. He had a genuine liking for his predecessor. "Fine old fellow, wasn't he?" was a not uncommon remark to his Secretary. Alive to the power and influence of the presidential office, he said to Cleveland as they drove together to the Capitol on Inauguration Day, "What an impressive thing it is to assume tremendous responsibilities!" [4]   And Cleve-

---

[1] Stanwood, ii. 386.   [2] Ibid., 391.

[3] Noyes, Amer. Finance, 269.

The Dingley Act reimposed the duties on wool; brought about a duty on hides that had been on the free list since 1872; imposed lower duties on cotton goods than those of 1890 but higher on silks and linens; restored the rates on chinaware of 1890. Iron ore was dutiable at 40¢, pig iron at $4, steel rails $7.84 per ton, the same as in 1894. Tin plate under the Act of 1890 paid 2⅖¢, in 1894, 1⅕¢, and in 1897, 1½¢ per pound. On sugar the differential was the same as under the act of 1894. "But the moral effect was very different. The House in 1897 had adopted the plan of leaving things as they were and had successfully resisted the effort of the refining monopoly to secure more." — Taussig. Tariff History, 5th ed., 328, 332, 335, 336, 342, 347, 352. See also correspondence in Life and Times of Dingley, 424 et seq.

"The Dingley Act restored the duty on works of art, free under the Tariff of 1894." — Tarbell, 243.   "European travellers could bring in free only one hundred dollars worth of goods bought abroad." — Dingley, 443.   "The tariff of 1897 like that of 1890 was the outcome of an aggressive spirit of protection." — Taussig, 358.

[4] Olcott, ii. 367.

land returned the liking and respect. "McKinley was distinguished, great and useful," he declared in his Memorial address at Princeton, "patriotic and faithful as a soldier, honest and upright as a citizen, tender and devoted as a husband and truthful, generous, unselfish, moral and clean in every relation of life."[1]

Cleveland and Olney had negotiated "a treaty for the arbitration of all matters in difference between the United States and Great Britain" which Cleveland had transmitted to the Senate during January, 1897, where it was pending when McKinley took the oath of office. Believing that politics should cease at the water's edge, he took the rather unusual course of approving emphatically a treaty negotiated by a preceding administration, which was that of a partisan opponent. "We want no wars of conquest," McKinley said in his inaugural address; "we must avoid the temptation of territorial aggression. War should never be entered upon until every agency of peace has failed; peace is preferable to war in almost every contingency. Arbitration is the true method of settlement of international as well as local or individual differences. . . . Since this treaty [the Olney-Pauncefote treaty of Jan. 11, 1897] is clearly the result of our own initiative, since it has been recognized as the leading feature of our foreign policy throughout our entire national history—the adjustment of difficulties by judicial methods rather than by force of arms — and since it presents to the world the glorious example of reason and peace, not passion and war, controlling the relations between two of the greatest nations of the world, an example certainly to be followed

---

[1] This address was delivered on Sept. 19, 1901, Andrew F. West, *Century Magazine*, Jan., 1909.

by others, I respectfully urge the early action of the Senate thereon, not merely as a matter of policy but as a duty to mankind. The importance and moral influence of the ratification of such a treaty can hardly be over-estimated in the cause of advancing civilization." [1] The Senate acted on the treaty but failed to ratify it, the vote on May 5, 1897, standing 43, to 26, less than the necessary two thirds. The result was a disappointment to the President and his intimate friends.

McKinley felt fully competent to deal with the tariff, which was one of the absorbing questions during his first months in the White House, and he gave efficient aid to the supporters of the Dingley Act. The Cuban question troubled him from the first. With Cleveland at the White House on the evening before his inauguration, he manifested the subject uppermost in his mind — the threatened conflict with Spain and the horrors of war. "Mr. President," he said, "if I can only go out of office at the end of my term, with the knowledge that I have done what lay in my power to avert this terrible calamity, with the success that has crowned your patience and persistence, I shall be the happiest man in the world." [2] Sherman's failure disturbed him, but during April [3] he called to his aid William R. Day as Assistant Secretary of State. Day had inherited his essential qualities from his father who was of fine subtle fibre all through and a retiring nature. [4] William R. Day was a fellow practitioner

---

[1] Moore, International Law Digest, vii. 75 *et seq.*
[2] Parker's Rec., 249.
[3] 1897. Day was nominated April 24. The nomination was not received in the Senate until May 3. He was confirmed on the same day.
[4] Riddle, Rec., 234.

of McKinley at the Canton, Ohio, bar, and was known by the President as one comes to know one's daily associates and competitors. The two now wrought together in entire harmony and, so far as one may judge by the diplomatic correspondence, foreign relations did not suffer from the defection of Sherman. Sherman, however, could not brook his relegation to an inferior place and he therefore resigned on April 25, 1898, leaving Day the nominal as well as the real Secretary of State.[1] For a long while McKinley thought that he could settle the Cuban question without war and that he would have the country at his back, but he was hampered in the choice of a minister to Spain. He wanted Seth Low, and he thought that he might have persuaded him to undertake the difficult job could he have induced him to visit Washington. His next choice fell upon General J. D. Cox, an admirable appointment, who for personal reasons was obliged to decline it. McKinley would have liked John W. Foster, but finally he named Stewart L. Woodford[2] whose work turned out much better than might have been expected.

From his inauguration to the assembling of Congress at its regular session in December, 1897, McKinley tasted the sweets of office. After the adjournment of Congress on July 24, he took a trip East, stopping at a hotel on the New York side of Lake Champlain. One day he crossed over into Vermont and was struck with the sturdy patriotism of the men of the Green Mountain State and their devotion to Republican party ideals. Returning to his own State, he paid a memorable visit to Mark Hanna,

---

[1] Day was nominated as Secretary of State and confirmed on April 26, 1898.

[2] Woodford was nominated on June 16, 1897.

whose hospitality he enjoyed for a number of days, meeting men connected with his administration and Republicans whom he looked to for countenance and support. Of a genial nature and possessing attractive manners, he commended himself to all sorts and conditions of men and, at this time, might sincerely have felt that his influence was second to that of no other man in the country.

CHAPTER III

McKinley's opinion expressed to Cleveland regarding his treatment of Cuban affairs was thoroughly sincere, and at this distance may be justified. "Patience and persistence" were well applied to Cleveland's and Olney's management. The Cuban insurrection began in February, 1895, and failed to be suppressed by a humane governor-general who conducted the war in accordance with civilized usage. He was succeeded less than a year later by Weyler, who adopted at once drastic methods, the most important of which was his proclamation requiring a concentration of inhabitants at military headquarters in the provinces still under his control. To require people to quit their plantations and villages where they might secure a living and herd together in towns subject to starvation and disease was extreme cruelty and deserved McKinley's statement that "it was not civilized warfare" but "extermination." [1]

During the spring of 1896, both Houses of Congress adopted a concurrent resolution declaring that in their opinion the United States should accord to the insurgents belligerent rights [2] but Cleveland and his Secretary

[1] Annual Message, Dec. 6, 1897. "The cruel policy of concentration was initiated February 16, 1896" — ibid. See The Relations of the United States and Spain, Diplomacy, Chadwick, 431. This valuable book will be referred to as Chadwick.

[2] The Resolution as finally passed, April 6, 1896, declared that the United States should be strictly neutral granting belligerent rights to both parties and that the president should offer the friendly offices of the United States to Spain for the recognition of the independence of Cuba. The resolution as passed was the Senate one. The milder one of the House was rejected by the Senate and the House receded.

of State Olney declined to act in accordance with this advice, not deeming that the insurgents had acquired a condition of proper belligerency. In his last Message to Congress, Cleveland told clearly the actual state of affairs. While Spain held "Havana and the seaports and all the considerable towns, the insurgents still roam at will over at least two thirds of the inland country. . . . If Spain has not yet reëstablished her authority, neither have the insurgents yet made good their title to be regarded as an independent state. . . . The excesses on both sides have become more frequent and more deplorable. . . . The rural population is required to concentrate itself in the towns." The industrial value of the island, consisting very largely in its capacity to produce sugar, was fast diminishing. In most of Cuba a state of anarchy existed, where property was no longer protected and life was unsafe. Despite the avowed sympathy of the inhabitants of the United States, the number of resident Cubans ready to help their brother insurgents, and the utter ruin threatening a neighboring and fertile country, our obligations to Spain, so Cleveland asserted, had been duly observed. But he uttered a note of warning when he said that a situation may be presented "in which our obligations to the sovereignty of Spain will be superseded by higher obligations." [1]

Reviewing carefully the last two years of Cleveland's administration, his conduct and that of his Secretary of State Olney in regard to Cuba merit commendation; they might easily have brought on a war with Spain.

The Cuban question was inherited by McKinley. The

---

[1] Message of Dec. 7, 1896.

Senate at the special session called in March, 1897, passed a resolution in favor of recognizing the belligerency of the Cuban insurgents, but it was never acted upon by the House, as Speaker Reed had not appointed a Committee on Foreign Affairs to which it should properly be referred. Anarchy in Cuba continued. In the destruction of property and disregard of life, the insurgents were equally to blame with the Spaniards. "The deliberate destruction of the support of a people," wrote Chadwick, "shown in the orders of Gomez [the insurgent leader] are deep stains upon the conduct of the Cuban cause." A large number of sugar mills were wrecked and this wreckage involved deprivation of work, and consequent suffering and death to vast numbers of working people. "Historic truth," Chadwick added, "demands the setting forth of the fact that Cuban and Spaniard were alike regardless of the misery caused by their methods and of its extent." [1]

During the summer and autumn of 1897, McKinley gave the subject much anxious thought which was apparent in his first annual Message to Congress. He referred with elation to the performance of its full duty according to the law of nations by the United States. The Government had "successfully prevented the departure of a single military expedition or armed vessel from our shores in violation of our laws." He argued against the recognition of the belligerency or the independence of Cuba and did not deem it wise to intervene for the present in the contest. Rather should we await the result of the entire change of policy promised by the new ministry in Spain.[2] The reactionary premier had been assassi-

---

[1] P. 524.   [2] Message of Dec. 6, 1897.

nated and Sagasta, a Liberal, had succeeded to the head of the new ministry which was in sympathy with his aims. When John Hay was first Secretary of Legation to Spain, he wrote in his Diary during 1869 : "Sagasta is the hardest hitter in the Cortes. Everybody calls him a scamp and everybody seems to admire him nevertheless. He is a sort of Disraeli — lithe, active, full of energy and hate." [1] A writer in the Encyclopædia Britannica said that Sagasta was a "leader, skilful in debate, a trimmer *par excellence*." He now appreciated in some degree, if not fully, the pressure from the United States. His ministry "recalled the commander whose brutal orders inflamed the American mind and shocked the civilized world ; it modified the horrible order of concentration and has undertaken to care for the helpless and permit those who desire to resume the cultivation of their fields to do so." It also proclaimed by decree a scheme of autonomy to become effective upon ratification by the Cortes.[2] It was extremely doubtful whether the Spanish mind understood autonomy as did the British and American, and a self-governing colony as was Canada could hardly be expected, but Sagasta was sincere in offering autonomy as he understood it.

It is easy to see that the President hoped for a peaceful solution despite the fact that the Sagasta scheme was not satisfactory to the extremists on either side. Riots occurred in Havana, which was loyal to Spanish interest, directed against the governor-general and autonomy ; owing to the prevailing excitement the United States Consul-General in Havana thought that it might be neces-

---

[1] Life of Hay, W. R. Thayer, i, 321.
[2] McKinley Message, Dec. 6, 1897.

sary to send a war-ship thither for the protection of the
American residents.   The President considered the matter and determined to send the battleship *Maine* to Havana, but the statement was made to the Spanish minister that it was "an act of friendly courtesy" and it was
so given out to the press.   Spain looked upon "the proposed visit of the *Maine*" as a proof of "cordial friendship," and replied that "wishing to reciprocate such
friendly and courteous demonstrations we shall arrange,
also, that vessels of our squadron may visit the ports of
the United States in passing to and from the island of
Cuba." [1]   While the President feared that the scheme of
autonomy had come to nothing, he nevertheless exhibited
his continued friendship to Spain.   At the diplomatic
dinner of January 27, 1898, he showed marked attention
to the Spanish minister and congratulated him on the
fact that "we have only good news." [2]

These friendly relations were interrupted by an indis-
cretion on the part of the Spanish minister in Washington,
de Lôme.   A confidential letter written by him during the
previous December to a friend sojourning in Cuba was
"surreptitiously, if not criminally obtained" [3] and, on
February 9, published by a New York newspaper.   De
Lôme said: "The message [the President's of December
6, 1897] has been a disillusionment to the insurgents
who expected something different; but I regard it as
bad [for us].   Besides the ingrained and inevitable ill-
breeding with which is repeated all that the press and
public opinion in Spain have said about Weyler, it once
more shows what McKinley is, weak and a bidder for the

---

[1] Spanish Corr. and Docs., 68, 69.   [2] Ibid., **71.**
[3] Day, Foreign Relations, 680.

admiration of the crowd, besides being a would-be politician who tries to leave a door open behind himself while keeping on good terms with the jingoes of his party." [1] De Lôme's folly was astounding. It was well known in Spain that while Congress was for war, the President was earnest for peace and no one could be in daily relations with him without feeling the sincerity of his purpose. The aim, therefore, of a Spanish diplomatist should have been to humor the President, not to impugn his motives. So far, however, as McKinley was concerned, he found most objectionable the intimation further on in the letter that the negotiations for commercial reciprocity with the autonomous government of Cuba might be "for effect" only. But as Assistant-Secretary of State Day wrote, "The publication of the letter created a good deal of feeling among Americans." [2] De Lôme at once cabled to Madrid his resignation which was promptly accepted. Day conducted the affair with discretion and on March 3 was glad to tell Stewart L. Woodford, our minister to Spain that the de Lôme incident was "fortunately closed." [3]

Meanwhile an occurrence took place in Havana which prevented the peaceful solution that the President sought. At forty minutes past nine on the evening of February 15, the *Maine*, lying peacefully at anchor in the harbor, was destroyed by an explosion with a loss of two officers and 258 men. The Spanish Government and the Cuban authorities expressed at once their sympathy with the United States on account of this dreadful occurrence, and their immediate action was all that could be desired.

---

[1] Foreign Relations, 1007.
[2] March 3. Foreign Relations, 680.   [3] Ibid.

The Court of Inquiry into the disaster was composed of three members and a judge advocate of the American Navy. Captain William E. Sampson was at its head and another member was Captain French E. Chadwick, whose excellent book on "The Relations of the United States and Spain, Diplomacy," gives an account of the transaction. "The situation," wrote Chadwick, "precluded any haste, and the inquiry was carried on deliberately, carefully, and searchingly for twenty-three days and with every effort to reach a fair and just finding."[1] The question in the official and public mind was, did the destruction take place from an external or an internal explosion? Chadwick was one of the two members of the Court who had thought the explosion was internal, and he and his colleague were convinced against their prepossessions.[2]

On March 28, 1898, Congress and the public were informed of the finding of the Court by a special message of the President to Congress. The Court determined that the disaster was not in any respect due to the fault or negligence of officers or crew. "In the opinion of the Court the *Maine* was destroyed by the explosion of a submarine mine which caused the partial explosion of two or more of the forward magazines. The Court has been unable to obtain evidence fixing the responsibility for the destruction of the *Maine* upon any person or persons."[3]

John D. Long, who at this time was Secretary of the Navy, in his book published in 1903, wrote: "The mystery of the loss of the *Maine* remains yet to be solved."[4] Chadwick, however, had keener insight, writing in his

---

[1] P. 543.   [2] Chadwick, 562 *n.*
[3] Senate Doc.   Destruction of Battleship *Maine*.
[4] The New American Navy, i. 144.

book published in 1909 that he "would welcome an examination of the wreck by a complete exposure of it as it lies. It could only result in substantiating the description of the injuries by the Court whose examination was too complete to leave chance of serious error." [1] Chadwick's expressed wish was gratified. In 1911, by a fine piece of engineering, the wreck was exposed and a board of one army and four navy officers made an examination of it, reporting on December 1, 1911, that the destruction was due to "the explosion of a charge of a low form of explosive exterior to the ship. . . . This resulted in igniting and exploding the contents of the 6-inch reserve magazine, said contents including a large quantity of black powder. The more or less complete explosion of the contents of the remaining forward magazines followed. The magazine explosions resulted in the destruction of the vessel." [2]

Contemporaneous material and many later books attribute much influence to Senator Redfield Proctor's speech in the Senate on March 17, which, owing to the confidence reposed in him by the country, held their attention. "My trip," he said, "was entirely unofficial and of my own motion." Of the six provinces in Cuba, "my observations were confined to the four western provinces which constitute about one half of the island. The two eastern ones are practically in the hands of the insurgents, except the few fortified towns. . . . All the country people in the four western provinces, about 400,000 in number, remaining outside the fortified towns

---

[1] Chadwick, 563 *n.*
[2] House Docs. 62d Cong. 2d Sess. No. 310.

when Weyler's order was made, were driven into these towns, and these are the *reconcentrados*. They were the peasantry, many of them farmers, some landowners, others renting lands and owning more or less stock, others working on estates and cultivating small patches; and even a small patch in that fruitful clime will support a family. . . . General Blanco's [the governor-general succeeding Weyler] order of November 13 last somewhat modifies the Weyler order but is of little or no practical benefit. . . . In fact though the order was issued four months ago I saw no beneficent results from it worth mentioning." "I am not in favor of annexation," he declared; and while Senator Proctor suggested no plan it is easy to see that intervention would have from him powerful support. "To me," he said, "the strongest appeal is not the barbarity practised by Weyler, nor the loss of the *Maine* . . . terrible as are both these incidents, but the spectacle of a million and a half of people, the entire native population of Cuba, struggling for freedom and deliverance from the worst misgovernment of which I ever had knowledge." [1]

The Spanish minister [2] in Washington was much impressed, telegraphing to the home government that Senator Proctor's speech had "produced great effect because of his temperate stand. He set forth in black colors the situation of the *reconcentrados*, declared that the country was opposed to autonomy and favorable to independence. . . . Before making the speech he had seen the President

---

[1] Cong. Record, 2916 *et seq*. Senator Proctor gave also the estimated population of Cuba with its racial divisions. He also discussed the military and political situations. Proctor had been Secretary of War under Harrison.

[2] Polo, who succeeded de Lôme.

and Day, for which reason more importance is attached to his words. My impression is that the President will try to withstand the powerful public sentiment in favor of the insurrection." [1]

As early as March 20 the President learned confidentially that the naval board would make a "unanimous report that the *Maine* was blown up by a submarine mine." [2] This knowledge and Proctor's account dictated Day's midnight telegram of March 25 to Woodford at Madrid: "The concentration of men, women and children in the fortified towns and permitting them to starve is unbearable to a Christian nation geographically so close as ours to Cuba. . . . It was represented to the President in November that the Blanco government would at once relieve the suffering and so modify the Weyler order as to permit those who were able to return to their homes and till the fields from which they had been driven. . . . The reconcentration order has not been practically superseded. There is no hope of peace through Spanish arms. . . . The Spanish government seems unable to conquer the insurgents. . . . We do not want the island. . . . Peace is the desired end." [3] Be it remembered that Congress, the country and Spain had the report of the Naval Board concerning the destruction of the *Maine* on Monday, March 28. Next day was submitted to the Spanish ministry what turned out to be the President's ultimatum. Premising that "the President instructs me to say that we do not want Cuba," Woodford said in conversation with Sagasta, with the Minister for Foreign Affairs and the Minister for the Colonies, who,

---

[1] Spanish Corr. and Docs., 95.
[2] Foreign Relations, 692.   [3] Ibid., 704, 712.

being well acquainted with English, acted as interpreter, "we do wish immediate peace in Cuba." The President "suggests an immediate armistice lasting until October 1, negotiations in the meantime being had looking to peace between Spain and the insurgents through the friendly offices of the President of the United States. He wishes the immediate revocation of the reconcentration order."

With effect, does Chadwick, in recounting the history of the diplomacy of these days, speak of Spain's "fatal habit of procrastination."[1] On March 31, two days after Woodford's conversation, she showed this in her answer to the President's reasonable request. Far from acceptance of the suggestion relating to the Armistice and consequent negotiations, it laid down propositions utterly inadmissible. Well did Woodford write to McKinley on April 1, "Yesterday's conference was a sorrow to me, for I have worked hard for peace."[2]

On March 30, the day between the President's request and Spain's answer, Day apprised Woodford of the state of affairs in Washington. "You should know and fully appreciate," he telegraphed, "that there is profound feeling in Congress and the greatest apprehension on the part of most conservative members that a resolution for intervention may pass both branches in spite of any effort which can be made. Only assurance from the President that, if he fails in peaceful negotiations he will submit all the facts to Congress at a very early day, will prevent immediate action on the part of Congress."[3]

It was evident that submission of the question to Congress meant a declaration of war against Spain. Public

---

[1] P. 554.   [2] Foreign Relations, 727.   [3] Ibid., 721.

sentiment had been worked up by the sensational press, frequently called the "yellow press"; it had manipulated the real news, spread unfounded reports, putting all before their readers with scare headlines. Newspaper editors and their assistants differed from those between 1850 and 1860, who made their appeals to the electorate by cogent editorials directed against the slave power. Now recourse was had to the news columns in which Spain was painted as perfidious and untrustworthy. After the Naval Board had made its report in regard to the *Maine*, it was impossible to convince the multitude that Spain had not, in some way or other, touched off the submarine mine which caused the explosion. "Remember the *Maine*" became the watchword. Appeal was made to what England would have done under like circumstances, whose "commonest phrase" was, "I wish you would take Cuba at once. We wouldn't have stood it this long." [1] Public sentiment acted effectually upon Congress, a dominant majority of which wanted war with Spain. "Every Congressman," said Boutelle of Maine, "had two or three newspapers in his district — most of them printed in red ink . . . and shouting for blood." [2]

It may be affirmed that if a referendum had been taken on April 1, 1898, a majority would have voted for war with Spain in order to expel her from Cuba. But the financial and business interests of the country were opposed to the war, as they deemed it needless and they shrunk from its horrors and expense. The Jingoes taunted men who held this view with being influenced by Wall Street, and it proved an effective taunt, but really Wall

[1] Life of Hay, Thayer, ii. 166.
[2] Oct. 22, 1898. Boston *Herald*, Oct. 23.

Street was only one part of this sentiment which was shared by business men throughout the country whose fit representative was Mark Hanna. "I am not," he declared, "in favor of heedlessly precipitating the country into the horrors of war" on account of the *Maine* incident or Spain's attitude to Cuba.[1] As late as April 5, he wrote in a private letter that in his opinion the Senate Committee on Foreign Relations ought to pass a resolution giving the President some discretion; otherwise, he added, "War cannot be avoided, and even under the most favorable circumstances it must come unless Spain backs down, which I believe she will do."

A phase of the reflecting and intelligent part of the community was well represented in the private letters of General J. D. Cox. "The dreadful accident to the *Maine*," he wrote, "ought to make everybody sober and reasonable in thinking of foreign affairs. It ought to be a very good cause that would justify a war in which such things might be happening any day. I don't envy the public man who should have to look back on an unnecessary war as in any part the work of his hands; and to rush into it for mere wantonness, as many seem inclined to, is such unspeakable folly as to make one wonder that it is possible in an enlightened age." Again, on March 2, "It is entirely incredible that a civilized government should have ordered or approved the destruction of a ship in her port in time of peace." And on March 29, "as to intervention, the whole island and everybody on it are not worth the American volunteers who would inevitably die of yellow fever if we sent an army there."

The officers and men who went forth to fight Spain,

---

[1] Interviews, N. Y. *Tribune*, Feb. 24, 27.

obedient to a dominant public sentiment and the fiat of
Congress, might have used the words with a variation
suitable to the time and country, which Philip Gibbs put
into the mouth of British soldiers who suffered and fought
in the trenches during the great World War: "I don't
want to die — I want to live. Why should I be sacri-
ficed to please the politicians of the world — those fools
who are the cause of all this? People at home don't
understand what we have to suffer. They don't care.
Those infuriated old females in England, those compla-
cent old bald-heads in St. James Street Clubs would see
us all smashed to pulp, and die to the last man, without a
question. They think it natural and nice, 'Dulce et de-
corum est,' etc."[1]

A phase of the sentiment of "literary fellows" was reflected by Theodore Roosevelt, Henry Cabot Lodge and
John Hay. "When the *Maine* was blown up in Havana
harbor," wrote Roosevelt in 1913, "war became inevitable."[2] He, in 1898, was impatient that the President did
not act more promptly and wrote in a private letter,
"The blood of women and children, who have perished
by the hundred thousand in hideous misery, lies at our
door; and the blood of the murdered men of the *Maine*
calls not for indemnity but for the full measure of atone-
ment which can only come by driving the Spaniard from
the New World. I have said this to the President before
his Cabinet; I have said it to Judge Day . . . ; and to
my own chief;"[3] and again, "McKinley has no more
backbone than a chocolate éclair!"[4]

---

[1] Boston *Herald*, May 4, 1919.   [2] Autobiography, 232.
[3] Letter of March 21 to Brooks Adams, J. B. Bishop. *Scribner's Magazine*, November 1919, 524.   [4] Peck, 642.

Henry Cabot Lodge wrote in 1899: "The outside engine of destruction [of the *Maine*] was a government submarine mine and had been exploded without the authority or knowledge of the Spanish government by men who wore the uniform of Spain. . . . The result had been inevitable since the fatal 15th of February, although men did not understand it at the moment and still thought they could stay the current of events which had been gathering strength for seventy years and broken loose at last." [1]

On May 8, 1898, John Hay, now our Ambassador to England, wrote in a private letter: "I detest war and had hoped I might never see another, but this was as necessary as it was righteous. I have not for two years seen any other issue." [2]

One may wonder if Roosevelt, Lodge and Hay took fully into account the Spanish habit of procrastination. Did Roosevelt with his habit of omnivorous reading come across the reported remark of Lord Clarendon: "Spanish dynasties go and come; Spanish queens go and come, and Spanish ministries go and come; but there is one thing in Spain that is always the same — they never answer letters" ? [3]

Senator Lodge of course knew all about Lowell's mission to Spain, and he might have read before the Spanish War his impressions of the people to whom he was accredited. "I like the Spaniards very well so far as I know them," Lowell wrote, "and have an instinctive sympathy with their want of aptitude for business."

---

[1] The War with Spain, 31 *et seq.*
[2] Life of Hay, Thayer, ii. 167.
[3] Life of Lord Granville, Fitzmaurice, 1905, ii. 31.

"They are unenterprising and unchangeable." "Spain is as primitive in some ways as the books of Moses, and as Oriental." "They fancy themselves always in the age of Charles V, and the perfect gravity with which they always assume the airs of a Great Power is not without a kind of pathetic dignity. We all wink at the little shifts of a decayed gentleman, especially when he is Don Quixote, as this one certainly is." [1]

John Hay in Spain, as first Secretary of Legation in 1869–1870, during the earlier insurrection, was impressed with her procrastination. Sagasta was one of the ministry and defended the government "with wonderful vigor and malice." "This government," wrote Hay in 1870, "wants to sell Cuba but dares not, and has no power to put a stop to the atrocities on the island. The only thing left to our government is to do nothing and keep its mouth shut; or interfere to stop the horrors in Cuba on the ground of humanity or the damage resulting to American interests." [2]

The pressure upon the President in 1898 to refer the matter to Congress was great. The Secretary of War, Russell A. Alger, said to a senator: "I want you to advise the President to declare war. He is making a great mistake. He is in danger of ruining himself and the Republican party by standing in the way of the people's wishes. Congress will declare war in spite of him. He'll get run over and the party with him." A bellicose senator said to the Assistant Secretary of State: "Day, don't your President know where the war-declaring power is

---

[1] Dec. 23, 1877, Apr. 14, 1878, May 2, 1879, Dec. 30, 1879. Letters of James Russell Lowell (1894), ii. 205, 213, 241, 246.

[2] Life of Hay, Thayer, i. 324.

lodged? Tell him that if he doesn't do something, Congress will exercise the power." [1]   Congressman Boutelle, who was opposed to the war, is authority for the statement that forty or fifty Republican members of Congress held a caucus, sent a committee to the President and told him that unless he sent an aggressive message to Congress, they would introduce a resolution for war and vote with the Democrats to carry it through.[2]   Olcott, the biographer of McKinley, is authority for the statement that the Vice President and a number of senators who were opposed to war polled the Senate in order to see if they could sustain a veto should a war resolution be prematurely passed; [3] but this must have been only a momentary thought, as for the President to veto a declaration of war by Congress was hardly to be considered.

McKinley was averse to war. He said to Senator Fairbanks: "It isn't the money that will be spent nor the property that will be destroyed, if war comes, that concerns me; but the thought of human suffering that must come into thousands of homes throughout the country is almost overwhelming." [4]   But he was much perturbed at the idea that his action might break up the Republican party. He could not sleep without sleeping powders. During the week when he sent what turned out to be his ultimatum to Spain he was much cast down but, on receiving her rejection of his terms, he determined to go with the war party and to turn the affair over to Congress. "Congress," wrote Senator Lodge, "has no diplomatic functions or attributes. With a foreign nation it has

[1] Life of McKinley, Olcott, ii. 28.
[2] Boston *Herald*, Oct. 23, 1898.   [3] Olcott, ii. 28.
[4] Life of McKinley, Olcott, i. 400.

but one weapon — the war power; and when a President calls in Congress in a controversy with another nation, his action means that Congress, if it sees fit, must exercise its single power and declare war." [1]   The President had decided to send his message to Congress on Monday, April 4; he postponed it until the 6th, then until Monday, April 11th, on account of an urgent request from the Consul-General in Havana to delay it in order that he might insure the safe departure of Americans from Cuba. On that day [April 11th] the message went to Congress: this action meant war with Spain.

No one can go through carefully the diplomatic despatches without thinking that up to March 31 McKinley's conduct of the affair had been faultless.   The pressure exerted upon the Spanish ministry and people was marked by courtesy, discretion and thorough knowledge of the situation.   John D. Long is the excellent authority for the consideration which McKinley and his Cabinet showed for the susceptibilities of the Spaniards. [2]   But just about as the President was to succeed completely he abandoned his policy and went over to the war party.   "To the people we come sooner or later," wrote James Bryce, [3] and the ministry of the cabinet government of Spain, though eager for peace, could go no further than they could count upon the support of public sentiment.   On April 3, Woodford telegraphed to the President: "The Spanish Minister for Foreign Affairs assures me that Spain will go as far and as fast as she can. . . .   I know that the Queen and her present ministry sincerely desire peace and that the Spanish people desire peace, and if you can still give

---

[1] The War with Spain, 36.   [2] American Navy, i. 133.
[3] American Commonwealth, i. 270.

me time and reasonable liberty of action . . . I am sure
that before next October I will get peace in Cuba, with
justice to Cuba and protection to our great American
interests." [1]

For the sake of clearness reference will again be made
to the President's ultimatum of March 27–29.[2] He demanded the immediate revocation of the *reconcentrado*
order and an armistice until October 1. The revocation
of the *reconcentrado* order was at once made. And now
the Pope, assisted by Archbishop Ireland of St. Paul,
who went to Washington by his order,[3] interfered in the
interest of peace. His intervention, supported by that
of "six great European powers," induced the Spanish
ministry to direct on April 9 the governor-general of
Cuba to grant immediately an armistice, leaving the
length of time to himself. Having submitted this action
to Day, Woodford telegraphed on April 10 to the President that if he could get full authority from Congress he
might secure a final settlement "before August 1st on
one of the following bases: either such autonomy as the
insurgents may agree to accept, or recognition by Spain of
the independence of the island, or cession of the island to
the United States. I hope that nothing will now be done
to humiliate Spain, as I am satisfied that the present
government is going, and is loyally ready to go, as fast
and as far as it can." [4]

The President and his immediate advisers had been
brought by the logic of events to see that no permanent

---

[1] Foreign Relations, 732.
[2] The despatch of Day to Woodford was Sunday, March 27; the submission of the ultimatum to the Spanish ministry, Tuesday, March 29.
The report on the *Maine* went to Congress on Monday, March 28.
[3] Spanish Corr. and Docs., 111, 112.   [4] Foreign Relations, 746, 747.

peace could be secured unless the Spaniards abandoned
Cuba; and in this they agreed with the war party. But
the Jingoes desired to smash Spain and were "spoiling
for a fight"; and the well-informed men of the war party
did not believe that Spain would give up Cuba without
war. But they could not see things as we see them now.
The Spanish ministry feared that a contest with the United
States would be hopeless. Whatever might happen
at first they appreciated that America had the "sinews of
war." The unanimous passage by the House of the bill
placing fifty millions at the President's disposal did not
excite the Spaniards but "stunned them." [1] On March
31, Woodford telegraphed to the President: "I believe
the ministry are ready to go as far and as fast as they can
and still save the dynasty here in Spain. They know
that Cuba is lost. Public opinion in Spain has moved
steadily toward peace." [2] "Speak softly and carry a
big stick," was Theodore Roosevelt's idea of a foreign
policy. Up to March 31 McKinley had spoken softly,
but after that he failed to continue the soft speech and
yet he had strong and what might have been efficient
support. The Speaker of the House, the Vice President,
all of his Cabinet but two, nearly all of the leading Republicans in the Senate were with him. [3] For it seems
clear that the Spaniards might have been led to grant independence to Cuba through negotiation. Jules Cambon, Ambassador from France, representing on the part
of his country financial and personal sympathy with

---

[1] Woodford, March 9. Foreign Relations, 684.   [2] Ibid., 727.
[3] Letters of T. Roosevelt to Captain Cowles, March 29, 30, 1898; to
Douglas Robinson, March 30; to Elihu Root, April 5; to Dr. Henry Jack-
son, April 6; J. B. Bishop; Scribner's Magazine, Nov. 1919, 524.

Spain, could see that she ought not to go to war with America, and labored to bring about a peaceful result. McKinley feared a rupture in his own party, and on account of that fear, had not the nerve and power to resist the pressure for war. We may rest assured that if Mark Hanna had been President there would have been no war with Spain. As much of a partisan as McKinley, he would have had the self-determination to resist the war party and the confident belief that he could secure the end desired without war and without the rupture of the Republican party; at all events he would have taken the risk.[1]

That the President had cast his lot freely with the war party was evident from his reply to the six representatives of Great Britain, Germany, France, Austria-Hungary, Russia and Italy, who hoped that further negotiations would lead to peace. We must end a situation, he said, on Wednesday, April 6, "the indefinite prolongation of which has become insufferable." [2]

---

[1] John W. Foster said at the Conference of the American Society for the Judicial Settlement of International Disputes on Dec. 15, 1910: "It is well known that President McKinley was strongly opposed to the war, and he was ably supported in striving for peace by General Woodford, to whom too much praise cannot be given for his conduct of the negotiations. It is now apparent that had not the President yielded to the war clamor in the country and the demands of Congress, the war might have been averted. . . . In the light of the Woodford despatches, we must conclude that President McKinley displayed the same firmness as Grant and Cleveland and continued to 'keep hold of the reins of diplomacy' the Spanish War with its long train of consequences might never have come upon us." See the Speeches of General Woodford and Congressman Boutelle before the Massachusetts Club, Oct. 22, 1898; Boston *Herald*, Oct. 23; Chadwick, 575; Remarks in the Senate by Senators Hale and Depew, May 25, 1908; Boyle's statement, Columbus, Ohio, May 25. Boyle was private secretary of McKinley when governor of Ohio, and afterwards his appointee as consul to Liverpool. Boston *Evening Transcript*, May 26, 1908; Boston *Daily Advertiser*, May 19, 1913; Conversations with Mark Hanna and Henry S. Pritchett.   [2] Foreign Relations, 741.

His message to the Congress on Monday, April 11, brought on the war. "With this last overture in the direction of immediate peace" [his ultimatum of March 27–29], he said, "and its disappointing reception by Spain, the Executive is brought to the end of his effort." [1] The disaster to the *Maine* was put in a subsidiary place in his message.[2] The President said toward the end of the message: "The issue is now with Congress. . . . I have exhausted every effort to relieve the intolerable condition of affairs which is at our doors. Prepared to execute every obligation imposed upon me by the Constitution and the law, I await your action." [3]

To the crowning effort of his diplomacy of being able to secure peace and in all probability Cuban independence, he referred in the last two paragraphs of his message in a perfunctory manner. "Yesterday" (Sunday, April 10), he said, "and since the preparation of the foregoing message, official information was received by me that the latest decree of the Queen Regent of Spain directs General Blanco, in order to prepare and facilitate peace, to proclaim a suspension of hostilities, the duration and details of which have not yet been communicated to me." [4]

Congress, the country and Spain knew that this message meant war. Congress immediately addressed itself to the subject and after certain disagreements united in the fol-

---

[1] Foreign Relations, 755.

[2] "In any event the destruction of the *Maine*, by whatever exterior cause, is a patent and impressive proof of a state of things in Cuba that is intolerable. That condition is thus shown to be such that the Spanish government cannot assure safety and security to a vessel of the American Navy in the harbor of Havana on a mission of peace, and rightfully there."

[3] Foreign Relations, 760.

[4] Foreign Relations, 760.

lowing resolutions, which were adopted on April 19, and signed by the President on the next day.[1] They said: "First. That the people of the Island of Cuba are, of right ought to be, free and independent.

"Second. That it is the duty of the United States to demand, and the Government of the United States does hereby demand, that the Government of Spain at once relinquish its authority and government in the Island of Cuba, and withdraw its land and naval forces from Cuba and Cuban waters.

"Third. That the President of the United States be, and he hereby is, directed and empowered to use the entire land and naval forces of the United States and to call into the actual service of the United States the militia of the several States to such extent as may be necessary to carry these resolutions into effect.

"Fourth. That the United States hereby disclaims any disposition or intention to exercise sovereignty, jurisdiction or control over said Island except for the pacification thereof and asserts its determination, when that is accomplished, to leave the government and control of the Island to its people." [2]

President Taft said that the Spanish War was an altruistic war.[3] The ground on which such a statement may be defended lies in the fourth resolution. It was offered by Senator Teller of Colorado and agreed to in the Senate without a division. It is wonderful that the United States, large and powerful, about to make war on

---

[1] The stages which led to these resolutions and the disagreements are well told by Henry Cabot Lodge in the War with Spain, 35 *et seq.;* see also Chadwick, 582.

[2] Foreign Relations, liv.   [3] John W. Foster, *l.c.*

Spain, weak and decadent, should renounce solemnly any desire to get Cuba. The fertile island, the Pearl of the Antilles, Cuba, had long been coveted by America, and now when the plum was ready to drop into her mouth she abjured the wish of conquest. But it seemed impossible to convince the Spaniards that our aim was not the annexation of Cuba. This resolution had the sympathetic adhesion of the President and many, if not all, of his warmest friends. It lightens up the declaration of this unnecessary war.

CHAPTER IV

NOTHING excites a nation so much as going to war. The first few days after its declaration, tumult reigns. So it came to pass in 1898. The feeling in Congress was intense and all the more so because it had been so long suppressed, awaiting the President's action. A large majority of Congress was in favor of war to expel the Spaniards from Cuba, and most of the Democrats, assisted by some Republicans, desired, as a stage in the proceedings, to recognize the republic of the Cuban insurgents. Two days after the President's Message was sent to Congress, the members of the House met in "a state of frenzied excitement" with "partisan passion running high." During a passionate colloquy, a Republican member said to a Democrat, "You are a liar," when the Democrat seized a bound copy of the Congressional Record and hurled it at his opponent. The missile fell short; the two members rushed for one another, and the House, so a reporter wrote, "was in an uproar. Shouts of anger and indignation were heard on every hand. Members in the crush espoused the cause of the two original combatants, and there were several exciting collisions but no blows struck." At last, owing to the work of the Speaker and the Sergeant-at-Arms, the efforts of a dozen muscular members and an impassioned appeal by Dingley, the fighters were restrained, the angry members took their seats "and a resemblance of order was restored." [1]

> "Beware of entrance to a quarrel, but being in,
> Bear't that the opposed may beware of thee."

In such wise did the McKinley administration conduct the Spanish War.

Congress formally declared that war with Spain had existed since April 21. Excitement had given way to alarm in the public mind lest the Navy might not prove equal to the job when the country learned that the first successful blow had been struck in the Orient on May 1 by the Asiatic squadron, under the command of George Dewey.[2]

During the autumn of 1897, Dewey thought that we were drifting into a war with Spain and, of all things, he desired the command of the Asiatic squadron. Theodore Roosevelt, in his position of Assistant Secretary of the Navy, had made up his mind that Dewey was the man for the place, but political influence was pushing another officer who was his senior.[3] "I want you to go," Roosevelt said to him. "You are the man who will be equal to the emergency if one arises. Do you know any senators?"

"Senator Proctor," [4] was the reply, "is from my State. He is an old friend of the family and my father was of service to him when he was a young man."

---

[1] N. Y. *Tribune*, Apr. 14; Recollections of Henry S. Pritchett.

[2] "The newspapers of May 2 had a brief announcement of the victory." Dewey, Autobiography, 228. These first (May 2) announcements were from Spanish sources and gave no adequate idea of the completeness of the victory; the reading between the lines made it possible to arrive at a conclusion that made the headlines of victory justifiable.

[3] Theodore Roosevelt, Autobiography, 231.

[4] Redfield Proctor, "who was very ardent for the war." Ibid.

"You could not have a better sponsor," Roosevelt re-joined. "Lose no time in having him speak a word for you." Dewey at once enlisted the favor of Senator Proctor, whose influence with the President secured him the appointment.[1]

In a Japanese harbor on January 3, 1898, Dewey took over the command of the Asiatic squadron and hoisted his broad pennant on the *Olympia*. In his accurate and modest account of his work, written soon after his return to Washington in 1899,[2] he told of the careful preparation that he made for an attack on the Spanish fleet in the Philippines. Before he heard of the disaster to the *Maine*, the news of which reached him on February 17, he had decided to take the squadron to Hong Kong. An evidence of the common working of two minds bent on war is Roosevelt's despatch to Dewey of February 25, 1898. "Order the squadron to Hong Kong. Keep full of coal. In the event of declaration of war Spain, your duty will be to see that the Spanish squadron does not leave the Asiatic coast, and then offensive operations in Philippine Islands."[3]

In Dewey's account of the interchange of hospitalities among the ships assembled at Hong Kong during the month of March, he related a conversation that he had with Prince Henry of Prussia, brother of the Kaiser, who remarked "that he did not believe that the powers would ever allow the United States to annex Cuba."

"We do not wish to annex Cuba," Dewey answered, "but we cannot suffer the horrible condition of affairs,

---

[1] Dewey, Autobiography, 168.
[2] Dewey, Autobiography, vi. This account was not published until 1913.
[3] Dewey, Autobiography, 179.

which exists at present in that island at our very doors, to continue, and we are bound to put a stop to it."

"And what are you after? What does your country want?" the Prince asked jokingly on another occasion ;[1] and, although a word in jest, it represented the European attitude which could see in our action only a desire to acquire a rich territory.

Having served under Farragut, Dewey looked upon him as a master. "Valuable as the training of Annapolis was," he wrote, "it was poor schooling beside that of serving under Farragut in time of war."[2]

On April 25 came this word from Secretary Long: "War has commenced between the United States and Spain. Proceed at once to the Philippine Islands. Commence operations at once, particularly against Spanish fleet. You must capture vessels or destroy. Use utmost endeavors."[3] Two days later Dewey set sail, on his 600-mile voyage to Manila Bay. The Hong Kong newspapers stated that Manila was impregnable, and in the Hong Kong club which was British, whose members were in thorough sympathy with the United States, it was not thought that Dewey would be successful in his attack. Arriving off Manila, he signalled for all the commanding officers to come on board his flag-ship and said to them, "We shall enter Manila Bay to-night, and you will follow the motions and movements of the flag-ship which will lead."[4]

That night (as he told the story) he asked himself,

---

[1] Dewey, Autobiography, 185.
[2] Dewey, Autobiography, 50.
[3] The New American Navy, Long, i. 182.
[4] Dewey, Autobiography, 206.

"What would Farragut do?" and he thought he would have done exactly as proposed.[1] On April 30 at 11.30 P.M., with all lights masked, the gun crews at their guns, Dewey entered the South Channel, and with eminent success ran by the batteries. After half of the squadron had passed, a battery opened fire but none of the shots took effect.[2] Now he was in Manila Bay in which was the Spanish fleet that he must "capture or destroy."

"In action," Dewey wrote, "we had six ships to the Spaniards' seven, but we were superior in class of vessel and in armaments." [3] Proceeding across the bay at slow speed at 5.15 in the morning of May 1, his squadron was fired upon by three batteries at Manila, two at Cavité[4] and by the anchored Spanish fleet. Still Dewey went forward to the attack, leading the column with his flag-ship *Olympia;* the rest of his command followed with a distance of 400 yards between ships. Two submarine mines exploded, but they were two miles ahead, "too far to be effective." [5] At 5.40 A.M., when two and one half miles away from their objective, the Spanish fleet, Dewey said to his captain, "You may fire when you are ready, Gridley." [6] At once the squadron opened fire. Firing without cessation as they moved, three runs were made from the eastward and two from the westward ; the length of each run was about two miles. Approaching on the fifth run, when nearest, within 2000 yards, this rapid

---

[1] Autobiography, 60.

[2] Dewey's report, May 4.   Appendix to the report of the Chief of the Bureau of Navigation, 70.   This will be referred to as Crowninshield.

[3] Autobiography, 203; see also 212, 213.

[4] Cavité was ten miles from Manila, had 5000 people, a navy yard, arsenal and fortifications.   Lodge, The War with Spain, 53.

[5] Report, Crowninshield, 70.

[6] Autobiography, 214.

and concentrated fire — "smothering," he called it —
demolished the Spanish fleet.   At 7.35 A.M., an erroneous
report was made to the Commodore that his ship was
short of ammunition ; this caused him to withdraw the
squadron from action, and gave his men time for break-
fast, as they had made the fight on coffee served in the
early morning.   All but one of the Spanish fleet, however,
had been destroyed, and as Dewey naïvely remarked, "Victory was already ours, though we did not know it." [1]   At
11.16 A.M., he returned with the squadron to the attack.
"By this time," he said in his report, "the flag-ship and
almost the entire Spanish fleet were in flames, and at 12.30
P.M. the squadron ceased firing, the batteries being
silenced and the ships sunk, burnt, and deserted." [2]   The
Spaniards lost at least thirteen vessels : three were sunk,
eight burned [only seven of these were in line of battle] ;
two tugs and a number of small launches were captured.
Their casualties were 381 men. [3]   In Dewey's squadron
none was killed and only seven slightly wounded.   "The
squadron," he reported, "is in as good condition now as
before the battle." [4]

"The completeness of the result," wrote Senator Lodge,
"which is the final test, gives Manila a great place in the
history of naval battles and writes the name of George
Dewey high up among the greatest of victorious admirals." [5]   The rapid and concentrated fire of the Americans
destroyed the Spanish fleet.   This disconcerted the Spaniards whose valor was remarkable but whose fire was
hasty and inaccurate.   Dewey told the secret of his suc-

---

[1] Autobiography, 218.   [2] Crowninshield, 70.
[3] Ibid., 71, 92.
[4] Ibid., 71.   [5] The War with Spain, 67.

cess. "It was," he wrote, "the ceaseless routine of hard work and preparation in time of peace that won Manila." [1] It looked " 'so easy' after it was all done." [2] But let one imagine Dewey with his Americans on the defence in the position of the Spaniards with their many resources and incentive to preparation, and let one conceive the Spanish admiral and his fleet the attacking party, and the result would have been just the contrary. But in truth the Spanish admiral would not have attacked, nor would any American of "the respectable commonplace type." [3] To attack a foe seven thousand miles from a base was a risk too great to take for any commander who did not pattern after Nelson and Farragut, as defeat or even "failure to gain a decisive victory" would have been a disaster.[4] Dewey was long-headed as well as daring and took into account all the conditions of the game. "In the event of defeat," he wrote, "no ship of our Asiatic squadron would have been afloat to tell the story." [5]

Honors and congratulations came. The President made him a rear-admiral. Congress thanked him, his officers and men. In writing to him, his "old friend" John Hay spoke of his "mingled wisdom and daring." Roosevelt, who appreciated Dewey before and admired him greatly after the battle, cabled, "Every American is your debtor." [6]

It was the "man behind the gun" that did the business. The Spanish Captain-General in his war proclamation

---

[1] Autobiography, 231.   [2] The War with Spain, 62.
[3] Roosevelt Autobiography, 231.
[4] Admiral Luce, cited by Dewey, Autobiography, 189 *n.*
[5] Autobiography, 252.
[6] Dewey, Autobiography, 229.

had declared that the North American people "were constituted of all the social excrescences;" their squadron was "manned by foreigners possessing neither instruction nor discipline." As a matter of fact, the percentage of American-born seamen in Dewey's squadron was about eighty all told. The Archbishop of Manila who, it was said, had written the Captain-General's proclamation, visited the *Olympia* some months afterwards and Dewey had the ship's company paraded in his honor. "As he saw the fine young fellows march past," wrote the Admiral, "his surprise at their appearance was manifest." "Admiral," he said, "you must be very proud to command such a body of men." "Yes, I am," was the reply, "and I have just the same kind of men on board all the other ships in the harbor." "Admiral," the Archbishop rejoined, "I have been here for thirty years. I have seen the men-of-war of all the nations but never have I seen anything like this," as he pointed to the *Olympia's* crew.

Dewey paid tribute to his officers as well as to his men. "I doubt," he said in his report, "if any commander-in-chief under similar circumstances, was ever served by more loyal, efficient and gallant captains than those of the squadron now under my command." [1]

The moral effect of Dewey's victory was great. It gave the country confidence in her navy. It was generally thought that on paper the Spanish Navy was supe-

---

[1] My authorities for the battle of Manila Bay are Dewey's account printed in his Autobiography; reports of Dewey, Gridley, Coghlan, Walker, Dyer, Wood, Wildes, Montojo, the Spanish Admiral, printed by Crowninshield. I have also used The War with Spain, Lodge; The New American Navy, Long; and I have consulted the Autobiography of Roosevelt; Twenty Years of the Republic, Peck; America as a World Power, J. H. Latané (Hart's American Nation Series); *The Nation*, May 5, 12, 1898.

rior, and it might prove so in action. As a formidable
fleet would certainly be sent across the ocean, imagination ran riot as to the destruction it might cause to the
seaboard cities and to the summer resorts on the coast.
Many Boston men took their securities inland to Worcester and Springfield. Roosevelt spoke of it as a "fairly
comic panic" and wrote truly, "The state of nervousness
along much of the seacoast was funny in view of the lack
of foundation for it." [1] For the authorities in Washington, naval and otherwise, had perfect trust in the American Navy and felt that with a fair show it would destroy
any Spanish squadron sent across the water to take a
necessary part in the war. Now Dewey's victory showed
the stuff in the officers and men of the American Navy
and imparted a confidence to the general public that was
sorely needed at the commencement of hostilities.

Sympathy in the large powers of Europe on the continent was with Spain, and especial manifestations were
in Paris and Berlin. If there was any design to interfere
in the conflict, it was checked by the attitude of England,
who favored decidedly the United States. Dewey's victory strengthened the position of England by rendering
any intervention on the part of the continental powers
impossible. Sentiment on the continent was that, in the
first encounters, Spain would be victorious, such was the
confidence felt in her navy and distrust in the American
sea power. Andrew D. White, our Ambassador to Germany, gave a vivid account of the sentiment, as shown in
the German newspapers and in an interview granted by
Mommsen, on the conduct of the United States toward

---

[1] Autobiography, 235.

Spain. This, White wrote, "was even more acrid than his previous utterances and exhibited sharply and at great length our alleged sins and shortcomings." [1] Following the Spanish newspapers, which liked to call their opponents "Yankee pigs," the "continental press teemed with the grossest caricatures, in which the Americans were drawn as swine." [2]

Anatole France in his novel "L'Anneau d'Améthyste" (226), published in 1899, gave this lively account of a conversation in a Paris salon: A general expressed the opinion that "in declaring war on Spain the Americans were imprudent and it may cost them dear. Having neither an Army nor a Navy it will be difficult for them to maintain a conflict with a trained army and experienced sailors. . . . The Americans are not prepared for war, and war requires long preparation."

"Now then, general," cried a lady, "do tell us that those American bandits will be beaten."

"Their success is doubtful," replied the general. "I should say that it would even be absurd, and would amount to an insolent contradiction of the whole system in vogue among military nations. In short the victory of the United States would constitute a practical criticism of principles adopted in the whole of Europe by the most competent military authorities. Such a result is neither to be expected nor desired."

"What luck!" exclaimed the lady, "Our friends the Spaniards will be victorious.   Vive le roi!"

"Certain facts seem to indicate that the Americans are

---

[1] Autobiography, 11, 160, 178. White saw the proof sheets of the interview but it was never published.

[2] Peck, 544, 553.

beginning to repent of their rashness," said a gentleman of the party. "It is said that they are terrified. They expect any day to see Spanish warships appear on their Atlantic coast. Inhabitants of Boston, New York and Philadelphia are fleeing in great numbers toward the interior of the country. It is a general panic."

A servant brought in the mail. "Perhaps there will be news of the war," said the gentleman opening a newspaper. Amid an intense silence, he read aloud: "Commodore Dewey has destroyed the Spanish fleet in the port of Manila. The Americans did not lose a single man."

"On the 30th of April, 1898," wrote Dewey, "I had been practically unknown to the American public. In a day my name was on everyone's lips. The dash of our squadron into an Oriental bay seven thousand miles from home had the glamour of romance to the national imagination." [1]

After the battle of Manila Bay, Senator Redfield Proctor wrote to President McKinley: "Dewey will be as wise and safe, if there are political duties devolving on him, as he is forcible in action. There is no better man in discretion and safe judgment." [2] The sequel showed how profoundly the Senator comprehended the Admiral. After the battle, Dewey established a blockade of Manila which he aimed to maintain thoroughly and impartially. A good student of international law, he was guided in his conduct by the best of authorities, and his attitude to the men-of-war sent by several nations to Manila Bay for purposes of observation, was correct. The English, who

---

[1] Autobiography, 289.   [2] Ibid., 228.

thoroughly sympathized with the United States, the Japanese, who partially did so, and the French, whose feeling was favorable to the Spaniards, respected Dewey's authority and permitted him to prescribe rules for their guidance. Not so the Germans, who were a law unto themselves and chafed against the exercise of any authority not their own.

After Dewey's return to Washington, at a dinner at the White House given him by the President, the President desired to know the truth of the statements frequently made in the newspapers regarding the friction between him and the German Vice-Admiral. "There is no record of it at all on the files," McKinley said. "No, Mr. President," Dewey answered, "as I was on the spot and familiar with the situation from day to day, it seemed best that I look after it myself, at a time when you had worries enough of your own." [1] Dewey came into collision with the Germans a number of times before the arrival of the Vice-Admiral von Diedrichs. On June 12, he came in on his flag-ship, the *Kaiserin Augusta* making the third German cruiser in the harbor; another was expected and a transport had already arrived. In accordance with naval etiquette, Dewey made the first call upon Diedrichs and referred to the large German force and the limited German interest in the Philippines. The British, with a much larger commercial interest, with a greater number of resident subjects, with the largest naval force of any power in far Eastern waters, never had at any one time during the blockade more than three warships in Manila harbor. To Dewey's gentle

---

[1] Dewey, Autobiography, 252.

remonstrance Diedrichs answered, "I am here by order of the Kaiser, sir." [1]

Dewey properly entitled his chapter "A Period of Anxiety." He had news of a more powerful squadron than his own on the way from Spain to the Philippines; he awaited with great anxiety intelligence from Sampson's fleet in the Atlantic; at the same time it was evident from the action of the Germans that they did not accept his interpretation of the laws of the blockade. They were on the most cordial social terms with the Spaniards in Manila, and the talk of the town was that the Germans would intervene in favor of Spain. Dewey addressed a formal letter to Vice-Admiral von Diedrichs in which he said : "As a state of war exists between the United States and Spain, and as the entry into this blockaded port of the vessels of war of a neutral is permitted by the blockading squadron as a matter of international courtesy, such neutrals should necessarily satisfy the blockading vessels as to their identity. . . . I claim the right to communicate with all vessels entering this port, now blockaded with the forces under my command." [2] To this Diedrichs demurred and notified Dewey that "he would submit the point to a conference of all the senior officers of the men-of-war in the harbor." Only Captain Chichester of the British ship *Immortalité* answered the call, and his expressed opinion was decidedly on Dewey's side. Nevertheless it took further and peremptory action on the part of Dewey to convince the German that his orders in Manila Bay must be obeyed. [3]

---

[1] Dewey, Autobiography, 257.   [2] Dewey, Autobiography, 265.
[3] My authority is ch. xvii. of Dewey's Autobiography. But see A. D. White, Autobiography, ii. 160 *et seq.;* Chadwick, the Spanish-American War, ii. 364; Long, ii. iii.; Lodge, 195; Peck, 578.

The glamour of our entrance into the Orient through Dewey's victory could not take the public mind, nor that of the historian, off the real centre of the war, which was in Cuba, and from the direction of affairs, which lay in Washington. On April 22, President McKinley proclaimed a limited blockade of Cuban ports, and four days later he declared "that the policy of this government will be not to resort to privateering but to adhere to the rules of the Declaration of Paris." On April 23, he called for 125,000 volunteers and a little over a month later for 75,000 more.[1] The Secretary of War, Alger, wrote that, as events turned out, the additional call was unnecessary, as 136,000 volunteers did not leave the United States.[2] But it is a tradition in American administration that Lincoln in his first call for 75,000 demanded too small a number, so that McKinley, if he erred at all, was bound to err on the safe side; but a prolongation of the war would have justified the larger number.

Before the United States declared war the President had appointed Captain William T. Sampson commander of the North Atlantic squadron. Advanced over seventeen other officers, he was made rear-admiral at the outbreak of the war and placed in supreme command of all operations on the Atlantic coast. Appointed rear-admiral sixteen days before Dewey, the appointment came to him as a surprise, causing him to feel deep responsibility rather than any elation.[3]

---

[1] Richardson x. 202 *et seq.*   [2] The Spanish-American War, 19.
[3] The Relations of the United States and Spain: The Spanish War, Chadwick, i. 18 *et seq.* Chadwick was Captain of the flag-ship *New York* and also Sampson's chief of staff. This valuable and useful work is in two volumes published in 1911 and will be referred to as Chadwick, The Spanish American War i. and do. ii.; see also The New American Navy, Long, i. 211.

The "sinews of war" were carefully looked after. Two hundred million of an authorized loan of double that amount was offered to popular subscription and eagerly grasped at. Although paying but three per cent, it was oversubscribed seven and one half times, was entirely taken at home and went to a premium of six per cent within three months.[1] A revenue bill was carefully framed by Dingley and his Republican associates on the Ways and Means Committee and adroitly piloted through the House and eventually the Senate; it became a law on June 13.[2]

It was known that a Spanish fleet under command of Admiral Cervera had left Cape Verde Islands on April 29, and was steaming westward. The public was uncertain as to its destination, but the Navy Department felt sure that it was either Puerto Rico or Cuba. As it proceeded much more slowly than was estimated, it was a source of mystification and alarm; it arrived at Martinique, a French island, on May 12, and one week later in Santiago harbor, Cuba. Cervera's choice of Santiago and decision to remain there made the battle, which finally took place, the decisive one of the war. In due time, his fleet was blockaded so that he could not make a sortie without a fight.

The President appreciated that to gain a decided result the Army must coöperate with the Navy, and Cervera's entrance into Santiago fixed that place as the Army's objective point. Consequently an expedition was prepared to proceed thither. Theodore Roosevelt, a participator in the war and the historian of a phase of it,

---

[1] Noyes, American Finance, 279.
[2] Life of Nelson Dingley, Jr., 462 *et seq.*

called the chapter on it in his Autobiography "The War of America the Unready," and this title is true so far as it applied to the Army. With the charitable and intelligent view of men and affairs, which was a real distinction in a man of active life, he wrote, "Secretary Alger happened to be Secretary when war broke out, and all the responsibility for the shortcomings of the Department were visited upon his devoted head. He was made the scapegoat for our National shortcomings. The fault was not his; the fault and responsibility lay with us, the people, who for thirty-three years had permitted our representatives in Congress and in National executive office to bear themselves so that it was absolutely impossible to avoid the great bulk of all the trouble that occurred, and of all the shortcomings of which our people complained during the Spanish War."[1] But it was different in the Navy, as no one knew better than Roosevelt, who was Assistant Secretary when the war broke out. "The Navy," he wrote, "really was largely on a war footing, as any Navy which is even respectably cared for in time of peace must be. The admirals, captains and lieutenants were continually practicing their profession in almost precisely the way that it has to be practiced in time of war. Except actually shooting at a foe, most of the men on board ship went through in time of peace practically all that they would have to go through in time of war."[2]

If one desires to read a graphic account of the bad management and confusion attendant upon our getting 18,000 troops[3] from Tampa, Florida, to Santiago, let him read

[1] The Autobiography (1913), 244.   [2] Ibid., 242.
[3] Chadwick, The Spanish-American War, ii. 77.

Roosevelt's books.[1] "We were kept several days on the transport," he wrote, "which was jammed with men, so that it was hard to move about on deck. Then the fleet got under way, and we steamed slowly down to Santiago. Here we disembarked, higgledy-piggledy, just as we had embarked. Different parts of different outfits were jumbled together, and it was no light labor afterwards to assemble the various batteries. For instance, one transport had guns, and another the locks for the guns; the two not getting together for several days after one of them had been landed. Soldiers went here, provisions there; and who got ashore first largely depended upon individual activity." [2] In some way or other the Army

[1] The Rough Riders; Autobiography.

Roosevelt went to Cuba as Lieut. Colonel of the Rough Riders of which Dr. Leonard Wood was the Colonel. In a private letter to Dr. W. Sturgis Bigelow of March 29, 1898, Roosevelt wrote: "I do not know that I shall be able to go to Cuba if there is a war. . . . But if I am able to go I certainly shall. . . . I like life very much. I have always led a joyous life. I like thought and I like action, and it will be very bitter to me to leave my wife and children; and while I think I could face death with dignity, I have no desire before my time has come to go out into the everlasting darkness. So I shall not go into a war with any undue exhilaration of spirits or in a frame of mind in any way approaching recklessness or levity."— J. B. Bishop. *Scribner's Magazine*, Nov. 1919, 531.

[2] Autobiography, 255. Roosevelt wrote in his diary which was given in 1921 by Mrs. Theodore Roosevelt to the Roosevelt Memorial Association: "June 3 — Reached Tampa in morning. Railroad system in wildest confusion; it took us twelve hours to get into camp with our baggage.

"June 5 —No words can paint the confusion. No head; a breakdown of both the railroad and military systems of the country.

"June 6 —No plans; no staff officers; no instructions to us. Each officer finds out for himself and takes his chances.

"June 8 —Told to go aboard transport. Worst confusion yet. No allotment of transports; no plans; utter confusion." — Boston *Herald*, Sept. 29, 1921.

Roosevelt wrote to his sister, Mrs. Robinson, on June 12: "It seems to me that the people at Washington are inexcusable for putting us aboard ship and keeping us crowded to suffocation on these transports for six days in Tampa harbor in a semi-tropical sun." Previously one whole night had been spent "standing up opposite a railway track waiting for a train to come, and finally taking coal cars in the morning."— Mrs. Robinson's Roosevelt, 169.

was entirely ashore by June 27.[1] The General in command was Shafter, a regular army officer of talent.[2] but entirely unfitted for a tropical expedition. Sixty-three years of age, weighing over 300, with a tendency to the gout, mounting a horse with difficulty,[3] his physical disabilities weighed upon him to an extent to unfit him entirely for his dangerous and responsible job.

"I expect to attack Santiago to-morrow morning," Shafter wrote to Sampson on June 30.[4] He was as good as his word, and the battles of El Caney and San Juan Hill resulted. The fort at El Caney was captured, but the fight at San Juan Hill was the more important. Captain John Bigelow, who was a captain in the regular cavalry with the expedition, wrote: "The enemy's position was about as nearly ideal as a real position can be. I have seen the famous stone wall at Fredericksburg backed by Marye's Heights. It is hardly a circumstance to this position. San Juan was more suggestive of Gettysburg than of Fredericksburg. Our attack seemed hardly less desperate than that of Pickett's division. At Gettysburg a cannonade of several hours' duration designed to shake the *morale* of the defence, preceded the advance of the attacking infantry which, during this period of preparation, was kept out of fire. At San Juan there was

---

[1] "The Army was in a region with a character wholly unlike that of any in its experience. Nearly the whole of the regular force of which it was composed had been accustomed to harrying Indians over treeless plains or arid mountains. In this case however it found itself in a country covered with brush so heavy that, almost impassable to the individual man, it was altogether so to troops in formation." Chadwick, The Spanish-American War, ii. 62.

[2] Chadwick, Spanish-American War, ii. 6; Alger.

[3] Chadwick, ii. 110; R. H. Davis, The Cuban and Porto Rican Campaigns, 185.

[4] Chadwick, Spanish-American War, ii. 75.

hardly any preparation by artillery, and the infantry and dismounted cavalry, who made the attack, were exposed to the enemy's fire for about an hour immediately preceding their advance, most of them not being able or permitted to fire back." [1]   The work was done by the regular troops, "the flower of the American standing army," Senator Lodge so termed them.[2]   They were assisted by three volunteer regiments, only one of which, the Rough Riders, under the command of Theodore Roosevelt,[3] did effective service.   The Cuban insurgents helped the Americans by doing their part in cutting off the supplies from Santiago, but were not as valuable support as had been expected.   San Juan Heights was taken on this July first.   "The attack," wrote Chadwick, "was indeed one of high heroism . . . as gallant a deed as was ever done." [4]

No word of praise can be too high for the work of the soldiers that day, but their creature comforts were not looked after.   They fought on empty stomachs, as the commissariat was badly managed; they were also short of tobacco so highly prized by soldiers in the field.   "Their woolen clothing," said Roosevelt, "was exactly what I

---

[1] Reminiscences of the Santiago Campaign, 127.

[2] P. 130.   Chadwick wrote: "Our first army was one of extraordinary quality; such probably as will never again take the field, as the conditions of its training can never be repeated.   It was the product of long years of war against the wiliest and most capable of savage races. Schooled in every trick of savage warfare, inured to every privation of heat and cold, individualized as no other soldier ever has been, these men of the plains were accustomed to fighting their own battles, and took with them to San Juan Hill the qualities and character which made this a force, which it is not too much to say, has never been equalled in general efficiency."   ii. 12.

[3] Wood had been advanced to a brigade command which made Roosevelt colonel of the Rough Riders.   [4] ii. 96.

would have used in Montana in the fall." [1]   The Spaniards were better armed and equipped and had a larger supply of smokeless powder.   Nevertheless, the events justified the charge on the fortified position, as Spanish firing was less deadly than the climate.   But the loss at El Caney and San Juan Hill was over ten per cent of the men engaged;   the casualties among the officers were unusually heavy.[2]

Next day, July 2, while the Spaniards made no attempt to retake San Juan Heights they kept up an incessant firing. This and the heavy losses of July 1 completely demoralized Shafter who, suffering from malarial fever, almost always accompanied by mental depression, was thoroughly despondent when, on July 3, he telegraphed to Washington, "I am seriously considering withdrawing about five miles and taking up a new position." [3]   Other officers of the army shared his anxiety but nevertheless two captains of the regular troops came to Roosevelt desiring him to protest against any retirement.   Roosevelt, who always disliked the word retreat, cordially agreed with them "that it would be far worse than a blunder to abandon our position." [4]   But Shafter had not forgotten the American game of bluff and at 8.30 that morning demanded the surrender of Santiago, which was peremptorily declined by the Spanish commander.

Senator Lodge gave a graphic account of the feeling in Washington on July 3.   "It was the one really dark day of the war," he wrote, "and the long hot hours of that memorable Sunday were heavy with doubt, apprehen-

---

[1] Chadwick, ii. 66.
[2] Chadwick, The Spanish-American War, ii. 100.
[3] Chadwick, The Spanish-American War, ii. 109.
[4] The Rough Riders, 148; Chadwick, ii. 108.

sion and anxiety." [1]   But if the administration in Washington and Shafter could have known the sentiment of
the Spanish camp, their despondency would have given
way to elation.   For Santiago was reaching the point
of capitulation; while the fleet had food for about a
month longer, the army and the city had been reduced
to rice.[2]   The fleet, however, was the important thing.
"The eyes of every nation," wrote Captain-General
Blanco to Cervera from Havana, "are at present fixed
on your squadron on which the honor of our country
depends." [3]   Before this Blanco had suggested to Madrid that all the land and naval forces in the Western
waters be placed under his supreme command and his
suggestion had been complied with.[4]   Admiral Cervera,
the commander of the Spanish squadron, was discouraged
at the outlook.   He wrote on June 25, eight days before
the dark day in Washington, to the Spanish general in
command at Santiago; "I have considered the squadron
lost ever since it left Cape Verde. . . .   To-day I consider the squadron lost as much as ever, and the dilemma
is whether to lose it by destroying it, if Santiago is not
able to resist, after having contributed to its defence, or
whether to lose it by sacrificing to vanity the majority
of its crews and depriving Santiago of their coöperation,
thereby precipitating its fall. . . .   It is therefore for
the Captain-General to decide whether I am to go out to
suicide, dragging along with me those 2000 sons of Spain."
On the same day he telegraphed to the Captain-General,
"In my opinion the sortie will entail the certain loss of

---

[1] P. 133.
[2] Chadwick, ii. 114.   [3] June 26, ibid., 119.
[4] June 20–25, ibid., 115.

the squadron and majority of its crews." [1]   Blanco desired the escape made "from that prison in which the squadron is unfortunately shut in" on a dark night and in bad weather, but to this Cervera replied, "With the harbor entrance blockaded as it now is, the sortie at night is more perilous than in daytime, on account of ships being closer inshore." [2]

Thus stood affairs until the army made the attack of July 1, after which the Spanish general in command reported the "exhausted and serious condition of Santiago." The result of that battle brought the Spanish authorities to a decision. Cervera had lent his "landing forces" to the army for the defence of Santiago, and to make a proper sortie he must have them reëmbarked. He received an order from Blanco on July 1 to reëmbark "the crews" and to hasten the sortie from the harbor. This was followed up by a despatch next day to go out immediately. A telegram to the general in command showed plainly the thought that dwelt in Blanco's mind: "Main thing is that squadron go out at once, for if Americans take possession of it, Spain will be morally defeated and must ask for peace at mercy of enemy. A city lost can be recovered; the loss of the squadron under these circumstances is final and cannot be recovered." [3]   It was impossible to make the sortie in the afternoon of July 2, so the morning of July 3 was decided upon.

The historian is able to look into both camps — a look of course impossible to either Sampson or Cervera. There was friction between Sampson and Shafter as well

[1] Chadwick, ii. 116, 118.   [2] Ibid., ii. 118, 119.
[3] Ibid., ii. 122, 124.

as between the Army and Navy departments in Washington. When the Naval Board announced — an announcement which was endorsed by the Secretary — that it was better to sacrifice a number of soldiers rather than to lose one battleship, such an opinion was regarded as inhuman although probably based on good naval strategy. Shafter, appalled at the losses of July 1, did not want to sacrifice further his men, and desired Sampson to force an entrance into the harbor on the Farragut plan, which, on his part, Sampson did not want to do on account of the risk of losing a battleship. Shafter was ill and telegraphed to Washington on July 3: "I have been unable to be out during the heat of the day for four days,[1] but am retaining the command. . . . I am urging Admiral Sampson to attempt to force the entrance of the harbor and will have consultation with him this morning." [2] This conference was to be had at Shafter's headquarters, for which place Sampson on his armored cruiser, the *New York*, started on the morning of July 3. The port at which he proposed to land was eight miles from his position in the blockading squadron. No fortune could have been worse for Sampson. Since June 1 he had maintained a perfect blockade of Santiago Harbor. "The faithful search-light" [3] made him feel secure at night. "When I wake up," he said, "and can see from where I lie the operation of the search-light, I can fall asleep quite contented, knowing that everything is all right." Among the eventualities which he considered, was the escape of

---

[1] On July 4, after the naval battle of Santiago, Shafter wrote to the Adjutant-General in Washington, "I am still very much exhausted, eating a little this P.M. for the first time in four days." Chadwick, ii. 192.

[2] Ibid., 109.   [3] Long, ii. 7.

ships from the harbor, and he had issued the order, "If the enemy tries to escape, the ships must close and engage as soon as possible, and endeavor to sink his vessels or force them to run ashore";[1] but he could have had no idea that the plan of battle which he had considered and carefully thought out would be put into force on that day. Not only was the commander-in-chief and his cruiser *New York* absent, but the *Massachusetts* had gone away forty miles in order to coal.

The Spanish squadron consisted of the armored cruisers *Infanta Maria Teresa, Oquendo, Vizcaya, Cristóbal Colón* and two torpedo-boat destroyers; the American, of the armored cruiser *Brooklyn*, the battleships *Texas, Iowa, Oregon, Indiana* and the auxiliaries *Gloucester* and *Vixen*. The Spanish vessels came out of the harbor of Santiago on this Sunday morning, July 3, "a superb day,"[2] between 9.35 and 10; the flag-ship *Maria Teresa* was in advance and, following at a distance of about 800 yards, were the *Vizcaya, Cristóbal Colón* and the *Oquendo* and at a greater distance the torpedo-boat destroyers. The men on the American ships were at Sunday "quarters for inspection," which was to be followed by divine service. But their officers were on the alert and, at the first sight of the Spaniards, the American ships, carrying out Sampson's standing orders, closed in and began the work of destruction which their careful labor of preparation and accurate firing enabled them to do. The Spaniards advanced with coolness and courage. The *Maria Teresa* "presented a magnificent appearance," wrote Robley Evans, Captain of the *Iowa*, and the fleet "came at us like mad

---

[1] Long, ii. 7.   [2] Wilson, The Downfall of Spain, 295.

bulls." [1]   At first the fire of the *Maria Teresa* was rapid
and accurate, but as the American fire "smothered" her,
it grew "ragged and inaccurate." [2]   "I felt sure," wrote
Cervera, "that the disaster was inevitable . . . although I did not think our destruction would be so sudden." [3]

Between ten and half past the *Maria Teresa* and *Oquendo*,
"with large volumes of smoke rising from their lower
decks aft, gave up both fight and flight and ran in on the
beach" when about seven miles from Santiago.   At quarter past eleven the *Vizcaya*, when fifteen miles from Santiago, "turned in shore and was beached"; she "was
burning fiercely and her reserves of ammunition were
already beginning to explode." [4]   Meanwhile the Spanish
torpedo-boat destroyers had been smashed by the fire
of the battleships and especially by that of the auxiliary,
Gloucester, a converted yacht.   Remained "the sleek
foxy *Colón*," [5] the "best and fastest vessel" [6] of the Spanish fleet, which was overhauled by the *Brooklyn* and
Oregon; at twenty minutes past one, forty-eight miles
from Santiago, she hauled down her colors and surrendered.

"I regard," wrote Sampson in his Official Report, "this
complete and important victory over the Spanish forces
as the successful finish of several weeks of arduous and
close blockade, so stringent and effective during the night
that the enemy was deterred from making the attempt

---

[1] A Sailor's Log, 445.   [2] Ibid., 446.   [3] Chadwick, ii. 138, 185.
[4] Admiral Sampson's Official Report, July 15.   Crowninshield, 507 *et
seq.*
[5] Spears, Our Navy in the War with Spain, 319.
[6] Sampson.

to escape at night and deliberately elected to make the attempt in daylight." [1]

President Roosevelt, with a comprehension of naval affairs such as few or no civilians had, after a careful review of all the facts, wrote, "It was a captains' fight." [2]

The casualties of the Spanish squadron, which numbered 2227, did not exceed 474 and were probably fewer; the American loss was one killed, one seriously wounded.[3] "It is safe to say," wrote H. W. Wilson, an English authority, "that most Englishmen, with their knowledge of 1812 and the feats of the Civil War, confidently expected the Americans to win. It is equally safe to say that no one anticipated that two important victories would be secured at the cost of but one American life. . . . After less than five hours' fighting a modern squadron was completely annihilated with infinitesimal loss and infinitesimal damage to the victors. It is the low cost at which victory was purchased that renders this great battle so honorable to the American Navy." [4]

The naval battle of Santiago was a great victory and decisive of the war. "Do not Europeans regard us as barbarians?" was asked of a man, who, though not a

---

[1] Crowninshield, 509.   Secretary Long wrote: "The battle of July 3 was actually fought and the great victory won in accordance with the plan of the commander-in-chief," ii. 8.   President Roosevelt wrote, Feb. 18, 1902: "Sampson's real claim for credit rests upon his work as commander-in-chief; upon the excellence of the blockade; upon the preparedness of the squadron; upon the arrangement of the ships head-on in a semicircle around the harbor; and the standing order with which they instantly moved to the attack of the Spaniards when the latter appeared." Long, ii. 208.

[2] Long, ii. 208.

[3] Chadwick, ii. 176.   According to Spanish authority the Spaniards had 323 killed and 151 wounded.

[4] The Downfall of Spain, 69, 334.

native American, had passed enough time in the United States to speak and write English well and, although devoted artistically to Europe, had gained a thorough comprehension of Americans. "They did," was the reply, "until you smashed two Spanish fleets, but they think so no longer." Such is the judgment of the civilized world. Our work toward the elevation of humanity, toward the greater diffusion of education, are counted as naught in contrast with these naval victories.

Noteworthy as was the victory of Santiago it was supplemented by humane action. "As the *Maria Teresa* struck the rock, the tars of the *Texas* . . . began to cheer." But their Captain Philip exclaimed, "Don't cheer, boys; the poor devils are dying." [1] When Captain Robley Evans instantly handed back the surrendered sword to the Captain of the *Vizcaya*, his "blue shirts" cheered lustily.[2] "So long," he wrote in his report of July 4, "as the enemy showed his flag they fought like American seamen; but when the flag came down they were as gentle and tender as American women." [3] "This rescue of prisoners," wrote Admiral Sampson in his report, "including the wounded from the burning Spanish vessels was the occasion of some of the most daring and gallant conduct of the day. The ships were burning fore and aft, their guns and reserve ammunition were exploding, and it was not known at what moment the fire would reach the main magazines. In addition to this a heavy surf was running just inside of the Spanish ships. But no risk deterred our officers and men until their work of humanity was complete." [4] Cervera in his report eulogized

---

[1] Long, ii. 39.   [2] A Sailor's Log, 451.   [3] Crowninshield, 539.
[4] Crowninshield, 509.

"the chivalry and courtesy of the enemy. They clothed the naked," he wrote, "giving them everything they needed; they suppressed the shouts of joy in order not to increase the suffering of the defeated, and all vied in making their captivity as easy as possible." [1] He wrote to the Captain of the *St. Louis* when "at sea" on his way home, "I thank you for the delicate and manifold acts of kindness through which you have endeavored to alleviate the sore burden of our great misfortune." [2] In other words, the American seamen fought like gentlemen and not like brutes. Exactly the same may be said of the American soldiers who contended before Santiago.[3]

As has been previously stated, the naval battle of Santiago was the decisive one of the war. Blanco thought that the squadron must make a fight to save Spanish honor but he recognized that its destruction meant that the game was up. The annihilation of the fleet, wrote Captain Concas, the acting chief-of-staff of Cervera, deprived "Spain of the only power still of value to her, without which a million soldiers could do nothing to serve her; of the only power which could have weight in a treaty of peace; a power which, once destroyed, would leave Spain, the old Spain of Europe, not Cuba as so many ignorant persons believed, completely at the mercy of the enemy." [4]

The fall of Santiago quickly followed. Puerto Rico was also captured. "In comparison to the Santiago

---

[1] Crowninshield, 562. See also Cervera to Blanco and Sampson. Chadwick, ii. 189, 190.
[2] Foreign Relations, 1898, 798.
[3] Chadwick, ii. 262; Peck, 598.   [4] Chadwick, ii. 128.

nightmare," wrote Richard Harding Davis, "the Porto Rican expedition was a 'fête des fleurs.'" [1]

Meanwhile it was learned that the reserve fleet of Spain was despatched to the Philippines, and soon thereafter an American squadron was collected, the destination of which should be the Spanish coast. This was publicly announced. The reserve Spanish fleet went through the Suez Canal, but the public announcement of the destination of the American fleet, together with the news of the destruction of Cervera's squadron, compelled its return to Spain.

A glance must now be had at the Orient. Troops were sent at different times until on August 6 there were about 8500 men ashore in the Philippines. General Merritt commanded the land forces and, in conjunction with Dewey, demanded the surrender of Manila and the Spanish forces in occupation. On August 13, an attack was begun which soon terminated, as arranged through "the good offices of the Belgian consul," by the surrender.[2]

The 10,000 Filipino insurgents under Aguinaldo had rendered valuable assistance in the investment of Manila and now made "a passing demand for joint occupation of the city" and, as the situation was difficult, Merritt and Dewey asked for instructions from Washington. President McKinley in reply directed that there "must be no joint occupation with the insurgents." [3]

"Had not the cable been cut," wrote Dewey, "there would have been no attack on August 13, for while our ships — counting the twelve hours' difference in time

---

[1] The Cuban and Porto Rican Campaigns, 296.
[2] Chadwick, ii. 408.
[3] Chadwick, ii. 423; Richardson, x. 217.

between the two hemispheres — were moving into position and our troops were holding themselves in readiness for a dash upon the Spanish works, the Protocol was being signed at Washington. The absence of immediate cable connection had allowed no interruption to the fateful progress of events which was to establish our authority in the Philippines." [1]

The smashing of the two fleets decided the war, and this was acknowledged by the Spaniards themselves. They had made resistance to save their honor but recognized that, when the fortunes of war decided against them, it was useless to prolong the conflict. Through a letter from the Spanish Minister of State to President McKinley [2] they started negotiations through Jules Cambon, the French Ambassador, who showed wonderful qualities. Frankly on the Spanish side, he saw clearly the American position, appreciated the magnitude of the naval victories and the helplessness of Spain. He found McKinley inflexible and disposed to drive a hard bargain. Believing that the "Conqueror resolved to procure all the profit possible from the advantages it has obtained," [3] he advised Spain to give him authority to sign the Protocol. This was done and the Protocol was signed by him and Secretary of State Day. [4]

The Protocol provided that Spain should relinquish all claim of sovereignty over Cuba, that she should cede to the United States Puerto Rico and an island in the Ladrones. This cession was in lieu of a pecuniary in-

---

[1] Autobiography, 282.　　[2] Olcott, ii. 59.　　[3] Chadwick, ii. 440.
[4] Elihu Root said when Secretary of War (Nov. 15, 1902) that Cambon was an " ideal ambassador," the " sympathetic representative and defender " of Spain. Miscellaneous Addresses, 145, 147.

demnity for the cost of the war. Furthermore, "The United States will occupy and hold the city, bay and harbor of Manila, pending the conclusion of a treaty of peace which shall determine the control, disposition and government of the Philippines."

Five Commissioners on the part of the United States and five on the part of Spain should meet in Paris not later than October 1 to negotiate and conclude a treaty of peace, subject to ratification by the constitutional authorities of both countries. This Protocol was signed on August 12 and involved a total suspension of hostilities.[1]

The war was over, having lasted 113 days [April 21 to August 12], less than four months.[2]

---

[1] Foreign Relations, 1898, 828.

[2] Authorities on the Spanish-American War: First, and foremost, the two volumes of Admiral French E. Chadwick. Chadwick has used the Spanish as well as the American documents with the result that he has enabled us to see both camps at the same time. He has written an impartial account. His action on the *New York* before and during the naval battle of Santiago made him an excellent interpreter of the documents, showing no animosity whatever to Spain. At the end of Vol. ii. he has given an excellent bibliography.

Reports of Battle of Santiago by Sampson; Schley and Cook of the *Brooklyn;* Chadwick of the *New York;* Clark of the *Oregon;* Philip of the *Texas;* Taylor of the *Indiana;* Evans of the *Iowa;* Wainwright of the *Gloucester;* Report of Cervera; Crowninshield, 506 *et seq.;* Autobiography of George Dewey; Foreign Relations, 1898; The New American Navy, Long; Lodge, The War with Spain; Theodore Roosevelt, Autobiography, Rough Riders; R. A. Alger, The Spanish-American War; Evans, A Sailor's Log; John Bigelow, Jr., Reminiscences of the Santiago Campaign; H. W. Wilson, The Downfall of Spain; R. H. Davis, The Cuban and Porto Rican Campaigns; F. D. Millet, The Expedition to the Philippines; Spear's Our Navy in the War with Spain; Mahan, Lessons of the War with Spain; Peck; Latané, America as a World Power, Hart's American Nation series.

Secretary Long wrote that the trip of the *Oregon* "has no parallel in history," ii. 54. Admiral Sampson spoke of her "brilliant record" under Captain Clark, Crowninshield, 510. "Her performance," wrote Chadwick, "was one unprecedented in battleship history and was one which will probably long preserve its unique distinction," i. 16. On "the *Oregon's* famous run," see Spear's chap. xii. For Hobson's exploit, see Chadwick, i. 338; Long, ii. 71.

CHAPTER V

In the first article of the Protocol, Spain relinquished Cuba. This rich island might fall to the United States. It was a ripe plum [1] that needed only the plucking. But there stood in the way the sentiment of a majority of the American people embodied in the so-called Teller Amendment to the resolutions adopted by Congress when the United States went to war with Spain. Although long a favorite policy that Cuba ought to belong to the United States, she now disclaimed any intention of taking the island, but proposed to leave it to the Cubans themselves. Any other large country would not probably in the first place have adopted the Teller Amendment but, even had it done so, its occupancy would have been made the prelude on one pretext or another to an eventual absorption. Undoubtedly a powerful minority would have supported McKinley in such a policy, but he deserves credit that, believing in the terms of the Teller Amendment when adopted, he held to them firmly, after the quick result of the war, and wrote a glorious page in his country's history as the pledge was faithfully carried out. In lieu of a pecuniary indemnity for the cost of the war and because it was desirable that Spain should quit the Western Hemisphere, Puerto Rico and other islands under the Spanish dominion in the West Indies were taken. Also on the ground of pecuniary indemnity an island in the Ladrones was required; this article resulted in the

---

[1] Substantially the same remark was made in chap. iii.

selection of Guam. Remained the Philippines, which caused much discussion in the Cabinet, country and with the Spanish Peace Commissioners, who by the terms of the Protocol, met in Paris those sent from the United States to negotiate a treaty of peace.

When the letter of the Spanish Minister of State was received [July 26] [1] the President on a hot afternoon took the members of the Cabinet on a lighthouse tender for a trip down the Potomac, when were thoroughly discussed the terms of peace. This resulted later in the submission by Secretary Day of an article which proposed to "relinquish all of the Philippine Islands to Spain except sufficient ground for a naval station." [2] On this proposition the Cabinet was about equally divided. It is easy to see that had the President then decided not to take the Philippines he would have had a powerful backing. During the war he had displayed a shrewd trading instinct thus expressed, "While we are conducting war and until its conclusion we must keep all we get; when the war is over we must keep what we want." [3] Now he did not desire to come to a positive decision, and preferred to leave the matter open for the development of circumstances and until we had more information and especially some enlightening word from Dewey. The President said to Jules Cambon: "The negotiators of the two countries will be the ones to decide what will be the permanent advantages that we shall demand in the archipelago and finally the control, disposition and government of the Philippines. The Madrid government may be assured that up to this time there is nothing determined à priori

---

[1] This is printed by Olcott, ii. 59.
[2] Life of McKinley, Olcott, ii. 61.   [3] Ibid., 165.

in my mind against Spain; likewise I consider there is nothing decided against the United States." [1] Therefore, Article III in the Protocol, agreed to with Jules Cambon, left the disposition of the Philippines until a formal treaty of peace should be concluded.

The Protocol provided for the appointment of five Commissioners to meet in Paris an equal number from Spain. The President named William R. Day, Cushman K. Davis, chairman of the Senate Foreign Relations Committee, William P. Frye, Senator from Maine, Whitelaw Reid, editor and proprietor of the New York *Tribune* and ex-minister to France, and George Gray, Senator from Delaware, the only Democrat on the Commission. The discussion between the Peace Commissioners and the different despatches of the Americans to Washington make interesting reading, but it is apparent that the decision of the main points rested with the President, who used the communications from the Commissioners as materials on which to base his own judgment. He decided at once that neither the United States nor any government which she might set up in Cuba would assume any portion of the so-called Cuban debt which had been largely incurred in fighting two insurrections.

The greatest contention, however, was in regard to the Philippines. These consisted of a number of islands with a combined area of 115,000 square miles, nearly as large as England, Scotland, Ireland and Wales. The largest is Luzon with nearly 41,000 square miles, substantially the size of Ohio. The total population was more than seven and one half millions; the population of Luzon was

---

[1] Despatch of Cambon to Spain, Aug. 4, Chadwick, ii. 436.

3,798,507 and that of Manila, the chief city, 219,928.[1]
"The Philippines were a rich prize for any ambitious
power," was Dewey's opinion after his victory.[2]

After the Protocol was signed, the President inclined
toward taking the Philippines. Of his five Peace Commissioners, three, Davis, Frye and Reid, were avowed imperialists. In his instruction to the Commission of September 16,[3] he wrote that we must have the island of
Luzon and on October 26 he had his Secretary of State,
John Hay,[4] telegraph as follows to Commissioner Day:
"The information which has come to the President since
your departure convinces him that the acceptance of the
cession of Luzon alone, leaving the rest of the islands
subject to the Spanish rule, or to be the subject of future
contention, cannot be justified on political, commercial or
humanitarian grounds. The cession must be of the whole
archipelago or none. The latter is wholly inadmissible
and the former must therefore be required. The President reaches this conclusion after most thorough consideration of the whole subject, and is deeply sensible of the
grave responsibilities it will impose, believing that this
course will entail less trouble than any other, and besides
will best subserve the interests of the people involved,
for whose welfare we cannot escape responsibility."[5]

---

[1] Life of McKinley, ii. 145; Foreign Relations, 1898, 925. "The entire population, according to the census of 1903, was 7,635,426. Of these
6,987,686 were classed as civilized and 647,740 as wild. The civilized native inhabitants are practically all adherents of the Roman Catholic
Church. Of the wild tribes at least two-fifths are Mohammedan Moros.
With the exception of the aboriginal Negritos, who are widely dispersed
through the mountain regions, all the natives are believed to be Malays."
Latané, 79.

[2] Autobiography, 251.   [3] Foreign Relations, 904.

[4] John Hay had become Secretary of State succeeding William R. Day.

[5] Hay to Day, Foreign Relations, 1898, 935.

Between October 10 and 22 McKinley visited the Omaha Trans-Mississippi Exposition; in going thither and returning he made a number of speeches at convenient rail stops.[1] Senator Hoar called it "his famous Western journey." [2] Unquestionably Hoar is correct in attributing to McKinley too great a reliance on the sentiment exhibited by the enthusiastic crowds that he addressed, but in truth his deductions from the meetings only confirmed what he had already determined.

By direction of the President, General Merritt went from Manila to Paris and gave a full report to the Peace Commission. While he was careful not to express himself positively in response to certain questions, a fair inference from his testimony is that it was desirable to take the whole group.[3]

The President had before him Dewey's report, from which it may be gathered that the Admiral favored the retention of Luzon alone, but General Greene, who brought to the White House this report, with whom McKinley had a "long talk" and whom he found "thoroughly well informed," approved decidedly our taking all of the Philippines.[4] The President had also

---

[1] For these speeches, see New York *Tribune*, Oct. 11–23, 1898.

[2] Autobiography, ii. 311.   [3] Foreign Relations, 1898, 918.

[4] "Luzon is in almost all respects the most desirable of these islands and therefore the one to retain." — Dewey, Aug. 29. General Greene said in his Memorandum of August 27 which represented his opinion when he had the "long talk" with McKinley on September 28: "If the United States evacuate these islands, anarchy and civil war will immediately ensue and lead to foreign intervention. The insurgents were furnished arms and the moral support of the Navy prior to our arrival, and we cannot ignore obligations, either to the insurgents or to foreign nations, which our own acts have imposed upon us. The Spanish Government is completely demoralized and Spanish power is dead beyond possibility of resurrection. Spain would be unable to govern these islands if we surrendered them. . . . On the other hand, the Filipinos cannot govern the

before him the opinion of the several members of the
Peace Commission before it was necessary to arrive at a
final decision. The opinions of the three imperialists,
Davis, Frye and Reid, tallied with his own; that of Day
was a compromise,[1] but Senator Gray's opinion deserves
consideration. "I cannot agree," he said, "that it is wise
to take Philippines in whole or in part. To do so would be
to reverse accepted continental policy of country, declared
and acted upon throughout our history. Propinquity gov-
erns case of Cuba and Puerto Rico. Policy proposed
introduces us into European politics and the entangling
alliances, against which Washington and all American
statesmen have protested. . . . Attacked Manila as part
of legitimate war against Spain. If we had captured
Cadiz and Carlists had helped us, would not owe duty to
stay by them at conclusion of war. On contrary interest
and duty would require us to abandon both Manila and
Cadiz. . . .

"So much from standpoint of interest. But even
conceding all benefits claimed for annexation we thereby
abandon the infinitely greater benefit to accrue from
acting the part of a great, powerful and Christian nation;
we exchange the moral grandeur and strength to be
gained by keeping our word to nations of the world and
by exhibiting a magnanimity and moderation in hour of
victory that becomes the advanced civilization we claim,
for doubtful material advantages and shameful stepping
down from high moral position boastfully assumed. We

---

country without the support of some strong nation." — Senate docs. 8, no.
62; Treaty of Peace between United States and Spain, 374, 383; Foreign Relations, 1898, 915, 917.
    [1] Foreign Relations, 1898, 932 *et seq.*

should set example in these respects, not follow the selfish and vulgar greed for territory which Europe has inherited from mediæval times. Our declaration of war upon Spain was accompanied by a solemn and deliberate definition of our purpose. Now that we have achieved all and more than our object, let us simply keep our word." [1]

Admiral Chadwick, after citing Gray's dissent, wrote: "There is no questioning the cogency of Judge Gray's argument, nor the nobility of its sentiment. To demand the Philippines was undoubtedly to alter the moral position of the United States and change its attitude from one of altruism to one of self-interest. This much is self-evident and scarcely requires statement." [2] But McKinley stuck to his determination and had Hay telegraph it to Commissioner Day on October 28: "The sentiment in the United States," he said, "is almost universal that the people of the Philippines, whatever else is done, must be liberated from Spanish domination. In this sentiment the President fully concurs. Nor can we permit Spain to transfer any of the islands to another power. Nor can we invite another power or powers to join the United States in sovereignty over them. We must either hold them or turn them back to Spain.

"Consequently, grave as are the responsibilities and unforeseen as are the difficulties which are before us, the President can see but one plain path of duty — the acceptance of the archipelago. Greater difficulties and more serious complications, administrative and international, would follow any other course. The President has given to the

---

[1] Oct. 25, Foreign Relations, 1898, 934.   [2] ii. 461.

views of the Commissioners the fullest consideration, and in reaching the conclusion above announced, in the light of information communicated to the Commission and to the President since your departure, he has been influenced by the single consideration of duty and humanity." [1]

On November 13, the President's idea was further elaborated by Hay's despatch again to Commissioner Day. "Do we not owe an obligation to the people of the Philippines which will not permit us to return them to the sovereignty of Spain?" he asked. "You are therefore instructed to insist upon the cession of the whole of the Philippines and, if necessary, pay to Spain $10,000,000 to $20,000,000. . . . The trade and commercial side as well as the indemnity for the cost of the war are questions we might yield. They might be waived or compromised but the questions of duty and humanity appeal to the President so strongly that he can find no appropriate answer but the one he has here marked out." [2]

The biographer of McKinley shows us the working of his mind in some words he addressed to his Methodist brethren: "The truth is," he said, "I didn't want the Philippines and when they came to us as a gift from the gods, I did not know what to do with them. . . . I sought counsel from all sides — Democrats as well as Republicans — but got little help. I thought first we would take only Manila; then Luzon; then other islands, perhaps, also. I walked the floor of the White House night after night until midnight; and I am not ashamed to tell you, gentlemen, that I went down on my knees

---

[1] Foreign Relations, 1898, 937.

[2] Ibid., 949. For an interesting account of the work of the Peace Commission, see Life of Whitelaw Reid, Cortissoz, ii. chap. xiii.

and prayed Almighty God for light and guidance more
than one night. And one night late it came to me this
way — I don't know how it was, but it came: (1) that
we could not give them back to Spain — that would be
cowardly and dishonorable; (2) that we could not turn
them over to France or Germany — our commercial
rivals in the Orient — that would be bad business and dis-
creditable; (3) that we could not leave them to themselves — they were unfit for self-government — and they
would soon have anarchy and misrule over there worse
than Spain's was; and (4) that there was nothing left
for us to do but to take them all, and to educate the
Filipinos, and uplift and civilize and Christianize them,
and by God's grace do the very best we could by them as
our fellow-men for whom Christ also died. And then I
went to bed, and went to sleep and slept soundly." [1]

It is true that McKinley was inconsistent in his public
words. In his message of December, 1897, he had said,
"Forcible annexation . . . cannot be thought of; that,
by our code of morality, would be criminal aggression." [2]
One cannot read the proceedings of the Peace Commission in Paris and see in any other light than that our taking of the Philippines was "forcible annexation." In his
instructions to the Commissioners of September 16, 1898,
he had said that the United States must be "scrupulous
and magnanimous in the concluding settlement." It
should not be tempted into "excessive demands or into
an adventurous departure on untried paths." [3] But our
attitude to Spain denied the injunction to show magnanimity, and our demand for and the taking of the

---

[1] Interview, Nov. 21, 1899. Life of McKinley, ii. 109.
[2] Richardson, x. 131.   [3] Foreign Relations, 1898, 907.

Philippines was an excessive demand and a venture on untried paths.

Yet McKinley was entirely sincere. He was truly religious, and when he told his Methodist brethren of the working of his mind, he told exactly the truth as he saw it. When he wrote, "The war has brought us new duties and responsibilities which we must meet and discharge as becomes a great nation on whose growth and career from the beginning the Ruler of Nations has plainly written the high command and pledge of civilization," [1] he meant what he said; and many good moral and religious men were entirely of his mind. Indeed it was a troublesome question to decide. The opinion of a majority of the American people was opposed to allowing the islands to go back to Spain; and yet as we see it now, that was the only alternative. They and the President did not believe that things should be permitted in the Eastern Hemisphere that they had gone to war to stop in Cuba. While the humanitarian impulse did the President honor, he had no right to commit his country to a dangerous course, to run the risk of "an adventurous departure on untried paths," on account of a religious sentiment. Despite the obvious opinion of the majority, which with "his ear close to the ground" [2] he well knew, his hold on the country was so great, increased as it was by a victorious war, that he could have led it to accept any conditions that he deemed necessary for the conclusion of a peace. The only possible alternative, leaving the islands to Spain, might have been done under conditions suggested by Commissioner Day. [3] Such con-

---

[1] Foreign Relations, 1898, 907.
[2] Peck, 659.   [3] Foreign Relations, 1898, 926, 934.

ditions would have filled the measure of humanity; but there would naturally have been the query whether Spain would or could carry them out.[1]

An American condition, however, should have influenced the President without fail. The Monroe Doctrine had come to be regarded as sacred and the spirit of it, if not the letter, was violated when we annexed the Philippines. We held that no European Power should take territory or increase what she possessed in the Western Hemisphere. In other words we said, "You keep away from us and we will keep away from you."[2] By the same token we were bound not to encroach on the Eastern Hemisphere. A cartoon in *Punch* entitled "Doctrine and Practice" represented Dame Europa in a garden, her attitude haughty, saying coldly to an intruder, "To whom do I owe the pleasure of this intrusion?" The intruder, in face, figure and get-up of the well-known type, replied "Ma'am — my name is Uncle Sam!" When came the rejoinder, "Any relation of the late Colonel Monroe?"[3] True it was urged that we had grown too large to be confined by the Monroe Doctrine, that the teachings of Washington, Monroe and John Quincy Adams applied to the country as it was then and had no longer application.[4] Others reasoned that the Monroe

---

[1] General MacArthur said in his Testimony before the Senate Committee on the Philippines on April 11, 1902: "When we landed [MacArthur sailed for Manila from San Francisco on June 27, 1898] we found the entire population [of the Philippines] in open, violent, vindictive resentment against Spain, as an expression of their desire to be emancipated from that monarchy. . . . I think if they had been granted the reforms which were extended to the people of the peninsula [of Spain] that the Filipinos would have been loyal Spaniards to-day." — Part ii. 1384.

[2] *The Nation*, Nov. 10, 1898, 345.

[3] *Punch*, Aug. 6, 1898; Winslow Warren in Boston *Herald*, Apr. 18, 1919.

[4] See *The Nation*, May 19, 1898, 376.

Doctrine only obliged us to keep out of Europe and had no reference to Asia.[1] But it was entirely easy for President McKinley to set aside such reasonings did he so desire.

The Secretary of State, John Hay, was influenced by the opinion of England as she had been the sole large European power on our side during the Spanish War. "The dull hostility between us and England which existed a year ago," he wrote while Ambassador, has been changed into a firm friendship. "If we give up the Philippines it will be a considerable disappointment to our English friends. . . . I have no doubt that Germany has been intriguing both with Aguinaldo and with Spain. They are most anxious to get a foothold there; but if they do there will be danger of grave complication with other European powers."[2]

With the determination of the President, events moved forward to the Treaty of Peace which was signed on December 10, 1898. It followed the Protocol as regards Cuba, Puerto Rico and the island in the Ladrones [Guam], but it further provided for the cession of the Philippine Islands and the payment by the United States to Spain of twenty million dollars. Neither the Cuban nor the Philippine debt was assumed. McKinley had a difficult time in getting his Treaty confirmed by the Senate which considered it from January 4 to February 6, 1899, and finally ratified it by 57 : 27, only one vote more than the necessary two thirds. Senator Gray signed the Treaty, advocated it in the Senate and afterwards accepted the position of judge from President McKinley. Naturally

---

[1] Latané, 259.
[2] Letters of Aug. 2, Sept. 9. Life of McKinley, ii. 135.

his after-conduct does not agree with the heretofore
cited opinion anent taking the Philippines; but in a newspaper interview and in his speech in the Senate for the
Treaty he explained his change of mind.[1]   Both Senators
Hoar and Hale, Republicans, opposed it, but Bryan came
to Washington during its pendency and urged enough of
Democrats to vote for it to secure its ratification.[2]

Two days before the ratification of the Treaty, the Filipinos, whose leader Aguinaldo was exasperated at the
non-establishment of a Philippine Republic with himself at the head of it, attacked the American soldiers at
Manila[3] and war began, which, with an ensuing guerilla
warfare, continued for more than three years.   In truth
the United States had paid twenty millions for "a white
elephant."   It was "scarcely comprehended," wrote
Dewey, "that a rebellion was included with the purchase."[4]   It cost the United States to subdue the Philip-

---

[1] Jan. 20, 1899; Jan. 31, Feb. 1, 1899, New York *Tribune*.

[2] Life of McKinley, ii. 139; George F. Hoar, Autobiography, ii. 322;
Latané, 77.

[3] The following I believe to be the truth about the much disputed question, who began the actual hostilities: "About 8.30 on the night of February 4, four Filipinos approached within five yards of an American outpost
near the San Juan bridge and, ignoring the command to halt, were fired
upon by the sentry.   A Filipino detachment near by returned the fire
and the firing soon became general along the entire line. . . .   The
Filipinos at that particular hour were unprepared for attack or defence.
The expected battle came when they were off their guard, most of the
higher officers being absent at Malolos." — The Philippines, Charles B.
Elliott (1916), i. 452.   J. A. Le Roy wrote: "The strained condition of
affairs between the American and Filipino forces, having reached a climax,
virtually brought on trouble of itself; a subordinate Filipino officer, un-
checked by the discipline of his superiors, was the chief *deus ex machina*
of the affray of February 4; the American authorities in Manila, having
taken a more positive stand at the close of that week regarding encroach-
ments upon their line, let loose the dogs of war they had been holding
ready, and promptly followed up the provocation given."   The Americans in the Philippines (1914), J. A. Le Roy, ii. 16.

[4] Autobiography, 284.

pine insurgents nearly one hundred and seventy millions,[1] while the cost of the Spanish War was three hundred million.[2] The one was attended with glory, the other with apology, despite the splendid results accruing from our rule.

Nearly all writers agree that the annexation of Hawaii [3] was brought on by the Spanish-American War, and by the taking of the Philippines. Hawaii, wrote John W. Foster, was a link in the chain of our possessions in the Pacific.[4] Like Cuba it had long been coveted by some American officials and a crisis occurring in January, 1893, furnished the fit occasion. "The Hawaiian pear is now fully ripe, and this is the golden hour for the United States to pluck it," wrote our minister.[5] A revolution, assisted by the United States forces, took place; the corrupt and despotic government of the Queen was overthrown and a provisional government established in its place. This government at once despatched a Commission to Washington with a treaty of annexation which had the thorough sympathy of President Harrison, who on February 14, 1893, signed it and submitted it to the Senate. The Treaty was favorably reported but, before action could

---

[1] Peck, 615; Senate docs., 57th Cong. 1st Sess. no. 416. June 20, 1902.

[2] Life of McKinley, ii. 112.

[3] "The Hawaiian Islands constitute a group of several islands in the mid Pacific having a total area of 6449 square miles. According to the United States census of 1900 their total population was 154,001 (or, deducting 274 persons in the military and naval service of the United States, 153,727). The latter number was made up of 61,122 Chinese, 25,742 Japanese, 29,834 Hawaiians, 7835 part Hawaiians, 28,533 Americans, 407 South Sea Islanders, and 254 Negroes." — Willoughby, Territories and Dependencies of the United States, 61.

[4] American Diplomacy in the Orient, 384.

[5] February 1, 1893. Pres. Cleveland's message of Dec. 18, 1893. Richardson, ix. 464.

be taken on it, Cleveland became President and during March, 1893, withdrew it; in his special message of December 18, 1893, he gave the reason for this withdrawal and for his subsequent action.   Believing that a grievous wrong had been done to the government of the Queen by the United States forces, he endeavored to restore her to her preëxisting power, but his movement was defeated by the recalcitrant action of the Queen herself.   With his sturdy sense of justice Cleveland could do no other than permanently to withdraw the treaty of annexation, but his attempt to restore the Queen was at the time unpopular and does not now merit approval.   As the United States would not have Hawaii and the Queen's government was impossible, the revolutionary parties established a republican form of government which was recognized by the Powers, including the United States.   This new government administered affairs "through a period of four years," so John W. Foster [1] wrote, "in which the country enjoyed unexampled peace and prosperity. Never before in its history had there been such honesty in administration, such economy in expenditures, such uniform justice in the enforcement of the laws and respect for the officials, such advance in education and such encouragement of commerce and protection to life and property." [2]

When McKinley became President Hawaii was annexed by joint resolution of Congress.[3]   This form was used as

---

[1] Foster was Secretary of State under Harrison at the time the treaty of annexation was presented.

[2] American Diplomacy in the Orient, 381.

[3] A treaty of annexation was signed June 16, 1897, and submitted the same day to the Senate, which body removed the injunction of secrecy on it the next day. — Senate Jour., 55th Cong. 1st Sess., 181, 183.

doubt existed whether a two-thirds vote for the ratification of a treaty could be secured in the Senate. "What is to be thought of a body," wrote John Hay in a private letter from London, "which will not take Hawaii as a gift and is clamoring to hold the Philippines?"[1] But on July 7, 1898, Hawaii became part of the United States by a two-thirds vote in both Houses,[2] a little over two months after Dewey's victory at Manila.

Had it not been for the foreshadowed policy in regard to the Philippines, it was a case of let well enough alone. A good government under a republican form was functioning in Hawaii and it was taking too great a risk to annex territory 2089 miles away.[3]

"The story of alternating 'booms' and panics," wrote Noyes, "is largely the story of modern industrial progress."[4] Those who believe in the periodicity of panics and recovery therefrom may note with elation that it was twenty years from the panic of 1873 to that of 1893, and twenty years from the "boom" of 1879 to that of 1899. As in the earlier case, recovery began sooner than was generally appreciated and is placed by Noyes in the middle of 1897.[5] Certain it is that the revival would have been in full swing had it not been for the Spanish War. War is a disturbing factor in finance and business and, when it was declared, no one would have dared to prophesy its brief duration. The "boom" year of 1899 resembles that of 1879. Both were the result of recupera-

---

[1] May 27, 1898, Life of Hay, Thayer, ii. 170.

[2] Foster, 383.

[3] Authorities: Foster; Willoughby, Territories and Dependencies of the United States; Cleveland's special message of Dec. 18, 1893; Peck.

[4] American Finance, 258.   [5] P. 262.

tive years after panics and both were attended with large
crops in the United States, a failure in Europe, or, as
Noyes expressed it, "A European famine and a bumper
crop at home," immense exportations of breadstuffs, an
import of gold and a buying-back of securities which
Europe had taken in former years. Hay and Adams in
their walks, discoursed of "the insolent prosperity of the
United States." [1] While the dominant characteristics of
1879 were an advance in the price of pig iron and railroad shares, 1899 was noted for its "boom" in industrials
and putting railroads on their feet.

John Pierpont Morgan is the hero of 1899 and of the
succeeding years, and he came into public notice from his
reorganization of railroads which had been badly hurt by
the panic of 1893 and by conditions prevailing before
and after. While circumstances favored his operations,
they were really marvellous and may be fully appreciated
by putting the question whether any other man in the
country could have accomplished what he did. Not by
affability and not by any strong hold on public sentiment
did he work his results; for he was reticent, taciturn,
decisive and blunt; his manner was stern and brusque;
endowed with great energy, he was ruthless. He lacked
a wide range of knowledge, but somehow he arrived
quickly at decisions involving millions to the amazement
of the beholder. He rarely read books and, on a constitutional question, he once displayed an ignorance that
would have disgraced a College freshman. But the
apologists for a mathematical training may point to Morgan as a shining example. From the English High

---

[1] Hay, Letters, iii. 140.

was President of the Carnegie Steel Co. and his report was to Henry Clay Frick, chairman, his superior officer, but both were under Andrew Carnegie, who, despite his obvious faults, was the greatest iron master of the world, was now at the head of the best equipped steel works and could make steel cheaper than anyone else.

"Between 1893 and 1899 our export of manufactures actually doubled." [1]

In the old school-books it was set down that the development of a State lay in commerce, manufactures, and agriculture. Agriculture was the largest single interest in the United States and commerce and manufactures owed more to it than it owed to the others. In 1899 the farmer was prosperous. "Every barn in Kansas and Nebraska has had a new coat of paint." "For anyone," wrote Ray Stannard Baker, "who knew the West of 1895 and 1896, with its bare weather-stained homes, its dilapidated barns, its farm machinery standing out in the rain, its ruinous 'boom' towns, its discontented inhabitants crying out for legislation to relieve their distress, this bit of observation raises a picture of improvement and smiling comfort such as no array of figures, however convincing, could produce. The West painted again: how much that means! The farmer has provided himself with food in plenty and the means for seeding his fields for another year; he has clothed himself and his family anew; he has bought an improved harvester, a buggy and a sewing machine; and now with the deliberation which is born of a surplus and a sturdy confidence in himself and in the future, he is painting his

---

[1] Noyes, 275.

barn. Paint signifies all of these preliminary comforts. And after paint comes a new front porch, a piano and the boys off to college." [1] Baker might have added that cancelled farm mortgages were reckoned by the carload.[2]

Since the campaign of 1896, there had been an enormous increase in the production of gold so that circumstances were ripe for the Republicans to fulfil the promises they had made in their platform of 1896 and during that lively canvass. Unquestionably the gold Democrats, who had supported McKinley, were disappointed that financial legislation was not enacted as the result of his victory, but those who believed in a protective tariff dominated the councils of the party and before they tackled the subject of finance they felt that the tariff demanded their attention: hence the Dingley Tariff Bill. McKinley and his immediate advisers had come to believe in a gold standard and were right in their conviction that a better law could be later secured than in 1897. But this conviction was based on the education of their party, as they could not have foreseen how Nature was going to work on their side.

On March 14, 1900, a law was enacted declaring the gold dollar to be the standard unit of value. It provided that "United States notes [greenbacks] and Treasury notes" issued under the Act of 1890 "shall be redeemed in gold coin; and, in order to secure the prompt and certain redemption of such notes, it shall be the duty of the Secretary of the Treasury to set apart a reserve fund of

---

[1] Ray Stannard Baker, The New Prosperity, *McClure's Magazine*, May, 1900, 86.

[2] In addition to authorities already cited, I have used *The Nation* for 1899, and conversations with Mark Hanna and J. P. Morgan.

one hundred and fifty millions in gold, which fund shall be used for such redemption purposes only." If that fund should fall below one hundred millions it should be the duty of the Secretary of the Treasury to replenish it to the maximum sum of one hundred and fifty millions. by the sale of three per cent bonds, of which the interest and principal should be payable in gold. The proceeds of these bonds should not "be used to meet deficiencies in the current revenues." United States notes, when redeemed and reissued, should be held "in the reserve fund until exchanged for gold." The legal tender quality of the silver dollar was unaffected.[1]

During the summer of 1900 affairs in China claimed the attention of the State Department, and Hay as its head directed the admirable course of the United States, showing great ability in state-craft.

John Hay, as he gave an account of himself, "was born in Indiana, grew up in Illinois, was educated in Rhode Island. I learned my law," he continued, "in Springfield and my politics in Washington, my diplomacy in Europe, Asia and Africa."[2] He had an innate sense of refinement but his cultivated manner never obscured his Western raciness. He loved society and talk. Residing ten years in Cleveland, he organized a dinner club, called the Vampire, of which he was the life. Hay used to come to the dinners primed with circumstances and anecdotes and, eating and drinking little, he gave himself up to talk and was listened to with interest and delight. Not infrequently one of the wits of the club

---

[1] U. S. Statutes, xxxi. 45.
[2] Life of Hay, Thayer, i. 2.

would prod Hay and, with his rare sense of humor a witticism of the sort served for an additional display. Occasionally he would fall into a serious strain and talk of political events or his acquaintances in New York or England, but always replete with intelligence. Sometimes, although with seeming reluctance, he would speak of his work on Lincoln, on which he was then engaged, and the business men, who gathered at that round table, were eager to hear of the processes of a live author. But it was a common remark that he never repeated himself.

> " What things have we seen
> Done at the Mermaid [Union Club of Cleveland] heard words that have been
> So nimble and so full of subtile flame."

"There is no longer the play of wit and raillery," wrote Professor Matthews, "the brilliancy, the concentration, the rapid glancing at a hundred subjects in succession, which there used to be in the attic nights of Johnson, Burke, Garrick and Sheridan." [1] But had the Professor dined with the Vampire, when Hay was at his best, he might have thought it an attic night.

Hay was the soul of the club and when in 1879 he felt compelled to accept the position of Assistant Secretary of State, offered him by William M. Evarts, he left a void, which, although the dinners went on, was not filled until his return to Cleveland, when he was welcomed with glee.

Hay was not a trained historian in the way of knowing thoroughly the masters of the art. He did not read with rapt attention Gibbon, Macaulay, Parkman or any other

---

[1] The Great Conversers (1874), 42.

historian except Henry Adams.   He was apt to have at
hand some high class French novel or Memoirs.   He was
especially fond of Tourguéneff. Is there in literature,
he asked, such another story of a suicide so dramatically
told, as that of Nejdanof in Terres Viorges?   During a
long acquaintance I never heard him talk of historians
except of his friend Henry Adams, but he had at his
tongue's end what we used to call belles-lettres and his
conversation thereon was a profit and delight.   In his
familiar letters written to his coadjutor Nicolay in regard to the History, when he spoke of condensation or
the troubles of narration, there is never a question how
Macaulay or Parkman would have treated the one or
solved the other.   We "must seize every chance to con-
dense," he wrote.   "We could cut down a good deal and
present what would be a continuous narrative in about
half the space we have taken for our book." [1]   Unquestionably had he followed out this idea, the History would
have been more popular and less criticized.

Although Hay did not possess the power of generaliza-
tion of Gibbon he had two qualities invaluable for a historian — that of narration and a skepticism that influenced in a marked degree his judgment of men and of
events.   And no writers in America ever had more price-
less material.   As private secretaries of Lincoln, feeling
that he was the central figure of the time, thinking that
some day they might write a history of these eventful
years, they made memoranda and garnered up their impressions.   Robert T. Lincoln, the President's son, had
a large body of material which he placed at their dis-

---

[1] Thayer, ii. 28, 35.

posal. The two merits which Gibbon ascribed as those of a historian, diligence and accuracy, they possessed. The ten volumes of the History testify to their diligence; that they rarely, if ever, failed in the correctness of a quotation or a reference is a warrant of their accuracy.

Hay was a partisan and he carried partisanship into his historical work, but he aimed at impartiality. "We ought to write," he said, "the history of those times like two everlasting angels who know everything, judge everything, tell the truth about everything, and don't care a twang of their harps about one side or the other." Yet in the same letter he wrote, "I am of that age and imbued with all its prejudices," and "We are Lincoln men all through." [1] Therein lay an unconscious partisanship. Nicolay and Hay made Lincoln out a saint and, when he came into contact with other men, the saint was always right.

"No man," Hay wrote in a private letter, "can be a great historian who is not a good fellow." A "good fellow," a genuine man was Hay in every respect.

An earnest Republican, he took great interest in politics and coöperated with the managers of the Republican cause in Ohio and in the country at large. Those who knew him best thought that, until McKinley appointed him in 1897, his ability was not appreciated by those high in power, as the offers to him of office were below his merits. He helped Hanna in the nomination of McKinley and when McKinley was elected, among the large number of well-backed aspirants for the English mission, Hanna's voice was for Hay; as Hay jocosely wrote,

---

[1] Thayer, ii. 33.

"Hanna is a good judge of men and he recognizes infalli-
bility when he sees it."   McKinley named him Ambassador to Great Britain, a position which pleased him im-
mensely and which he was abundantly qualified to fill.

McKinley and Hay took to one another, drawn together by an innate sense of refinement, for McKinley
appreciated culture. Hay was decidedly a cultivated
man. His natural propensity for culture was fostered
by the reading of books and by mingling in the best
society. Having a notable aptitude for acquiring knowledge at second hand he used this knowledge in his talk
with wonderful skill. Always meeting interesting people he absorbed incidents that in turn set off his own conversation. He loved wit and humor and any manifestation of them was to his latest day a passport to his favor.
He was a remarkable dinner-table talker and, in a discussion of the subject, a man of wide experience could
think only of two shining lights of Boston and Cambridge
who were his equal or superior.

In August, 1898, McKinley offered Hay the position of
Secretary of State for which he had no wish, as he would
have preferred to remain Ambassador to Great Britain.[1]
Thus he wrote during September to his brother-in-law:
"I did not want the place and was greatly grieved and
shocked when it came — but of course I could not refuse
to do the best I could. It was impossible, after the President had been so generous, to pick and choose, and say,
'I will have this and not that.' But I look forward to the
next year with gloomy forebodings." [2]

---

[1] The Education of Henry Adams, 364; Life of Hay, Thayer, ii. 173
et seq.
[2] Thayer, ii. 183.

The correspondence between McKinley and Hay, when Hay's first canal treaty was rejected by the Senate, is honorable to them both. Hay showed consideration for the President in offering his resignation and McKinley in declining it, affirmed his loyalty to his Secretary of State. "Your administration of the State Department," he wrote, "has had my warm approval. As in all matters you have taken my counsel, I will cheerfully bear whatever criticism or condemnation may come."[1] In his sympathetic eulogy delivered before the Congress, Hay rose to a sublime height, as he depicted the ability, moral greatness and success of his master. His countenance was the picture of his mind and heart. "His face," he said, "was cast in a classic mold; you see faces like it in antique marble, in the galleries of the Vatican; . . . his voice was the voice of the perfect orator."[2]

China, devoted to Oriental civilization, did not wish for Western modern improvements, had no desire for railroads and telegraphs, the importation of English and American cotton fabrics and of American petroleum. She could see no use in them; they disturbed her calculations and her mode of life; she was satisfied to be let alone. To the European nations she seemed inert — a fat goose for the plucking — and therefore, on one account and another, these foreign nations claimed and obtained "spheres of influence or interest." Especially was this the case with Great Britain, Germany and Russia, and, from their point of view, such spheres in China were economically and politically like their own territory. The China trade was important to the United

---

[1] Thayer, ii. 228.
[2] Memorial Address, Feb. 27, 1902.

States and the American manufacturers desired part of the consumption of the three hundred and fifty million Chinese. Did these nations adopt preferential tariffs in their spheres of interest, the American manufacturers would suffer, and for aid they looked to the State Department which was alive to the situation.

On September 6, 1899, Hay addressed a note to Great Britain in which his English predilection tallied with her traditional and declared policy for freedom of trade, and he asked her to maintain the "open door" policy which meant that the commerce and navigation of the world should receive equality of treatment within the "spheres of influence or interest." On the same day, he addressed notes to Germany and Russia pleading to these protective tariff countries for the "open door" policy within their spheres of interest, although to them he did not use the term "open door." On November 30 England replied that she would declare for the "open door" provided that the other powers concerned would do likewise. During December Germany and Russia answered, affirming the principle under like conditions. Meanwhile Hay addressed similar notes to Japan, France and Italy, from all of whom he received satisfactory answers. This led to his note of March 20, 1900, to the several six nations, giving the course of his negotiations and saying that as each nation had "accepted the declaration suggested by the United States concerning foreign trade in China" he considered the assent of each one addressed "as final and definitive." [1] Hay's sanguine anticipations were substantially realized.

---

[1] Corr. concerning Amer. Commercial Rights in China, Foreign Relations, 1899.

But the game of grab had received a check. The worm trodden on will turn. Before 1900, there were mutterings of the coming storm which is known as the Boxer uprising. The Boxers were a secret Chinese society and their name may be freely translated as "The Fist of Righteous Harmony." Sir Robert Hart "looked upon the Boxer movement as a national and patriotic one for freeing China of the foreigners to whom, rightly or wrongly, is attributed all the country's misfortunes during the last half century." [1]   Hart was properly called by the Encyclopædia Britannica, an Anglo-Chinese statesman and his remark was made after the suppression of the uprising which had individually cost him much; it stated a condition that the Boxers, dominated by the fanatics, sought to remedy, but the remedy was worse than the disease. The Empress Dowager who sympathized with the fanatical Boxers said in a secret edict, "The various powers cast upon us looks of tigerlike voracity, hustling each other in their endeavors to be the first to seize upon our innermost territories." [2]   A Chinese politician declared that the Boxer movement "was due to the deep-seated hatred of the Chinese people towards foreigners. China had been oppressed, trampled upon, coerced, cajoled, her territory taken, her usages flouted." [3]   While this feeling against foreigners as such was undoubtedly the main cause of the Boxer uprising, it was mixed with antagonism toward Christian missionaries who were trying to convert the Chinese to an alien religion.   Material conditions likewise fostered the movement.   In De-

---

[1] Foreign Relations, 1900, 207.
[2] Nov. 21, 1899.   Foreign Relations, 1900, 85.
[3] J. W. Foster, Amer. Diplomacy in the Orient, 416.

cember, 1899, our minister E. H. Conger wrote to John
Hay, "Crops have failed on account of the drought;
great poverty and want prevail." [1]   Little wonder was it
that a placard was issued saying, "The Roman Catholic
and Protestant religions have ruined and destroyed
Buddhism. Their adherents . . . have irritated heaven
and in consequence no rain has fallen. . . . If foreigners
are not swept away no rain will fall." [2] Swayed by these
different impulses the Peking Boxers attacked the foreign
legations.   On June 11, 1900, Conger wrote to Hay: "We
are besieged in Peking, entirely cut off from outside communication. . . . In a civilized country of course there
would be no question as to our safety, but here, with practically no government, and the army only a mutinous
horde of savage ruffians, there can be no predicting what
they may attempt." [3]   Ordinarily, government soldiers
would protect foreign legations but in this case the armed
Boxers, who were looked upon as patriots, were assisted
by the Imperial troops.   The entire city of Peking, wrote
Conger on June 15, is "in the possession of a rioting, mur-
dering mob, with no visible effort being made by the government in any way to restrain it." [4]   Five days later
the German Minister, who had ventured out on an official
errand, was murdered.   Nearly all the foreigners repaired
to the British legation, which was made a veritable for-
tress; their lines of defence were quickly shortened and
straightened; trenches and barricades were built.   "The
Chinese army," related Conger on August 17 after relief
came, "had turned out against us; the whole quarter of

---

[1] Dec. 7, 1899. Foreign Relations, 1900, 77.
[2] Apr. 30, 1900. Foreign Relations, 123.   [3] Ibid., 145.
[4] Foreign Relations, 154.

the city in which the legations are situated was surrounded by its soldiers, firing began on all sides and the battle against the representatives of all foreign governments in China was begun. . . . Until July 17 there was scarcely an hour during which there was not firing upon some part of our lines . . . varying from a single shot to a general and continuous attack along the whole line. Artillery was planted on all sides of us." [1]

Culminating by July 17, a thrill of horror ran through Europe and the United States at the idea that the legations to an ostensibly friendly country were besieged and in danger of massacre. London, Paris and Berlin believing that the worst had happened, mourned for those who had suffered this conjectured untimely fate. On July 16 it was stated in the House of Commons that the government entertained "no further hope for the safety of the foreign community in Peking." The London *Times*, the most conspicuous journal in Europe, which contained this news, printed in the same issue conventional eulogies of the British Minister, of the *Times* correspondent and of Sir Robert Hart, and gave a list of British officials and others who were in the Chinese capital. While those connected with the American press were inclined to the belief of their confrères over the sea, the Chinese Minister in Washington, Wu, Secretary John Hay and President McKinley doubted the story of a general massacre. Amid a period of excitement Hay and McKinley did not lose their heads and coöperated in efforts to relieve the suffering garrison. Hay was determined to get correct news and through Minister Wu sent a des-

---

[1] Foreign Relations, 162.

patch to Conger on July 11, "Communicate tidings bearer." Conger replied under date of July 16, received in Washington four days later: "For one month we have been besieged in British legation under continued shot and shell from Chinese troops. Quick relief only can prevent general massacre." [1] Five days later (not received in Washington until August 5) Conger telegraphed through the Consul-General at Shanghai: "All well. No fighting since 16th by agreement. Enough provisions; little ammunition. Hope for speedy relief." [2] In his despatch of July 21, Conger was somewhat too optimistic as the situation was one of ebb and flow. Nevertheless relief was at hand and he had the satisfaction of announcing on August 14, "We are safe." [3]

The occupying forces [4] restored order and organized a provincial administration, which gave way eventually to a reëstablished Chinese government. Protracted negotiations followed, with the result that suitable punishment was meted out to the guilty and an indemnity in a lump sum agreed upon. The success of President McKinley and Secretary Hay lay in their confidence in the Southern viceroys. As Hay said in his eulogy on McKin-

---

[1] Foreign Relations, 155, 156. "Your telegram was the first communication received by anyone from outside since the siege began and mine the first sent out." Conger to Hay, ibid., 161.

[2] Ibid., 156.

[3] Ibid., 160. The paraphrase of Conger's message of Aug. 17 ran: "Excepting the Imperial palace the entire city is occupied by 2000 Americans, 2000 British, 3000 Russians, 8000 Japanese and 200 French and is being apportioned for police supervision. The Chinese army has fled. The Imperial family and court have gone westward. . . . There are no representatives of the Chinese government in sight. The palace will be taken at once. . . . Conditions chaotic." It must be noted that our rapid action of relief was due to our having troops in the Philippines.

[4] For what the occupying forces were which relieved the foreign community in Peking, see note 3.

ley, "While the legations were fighting for their lives against bands of infuriated fanatics, the President decided that we were at peace with China; and while that conclusion did not hinder him from taking the most energetic measures to rescue our imperilled citizens, it enabled him to maintain close and friendly relations with the wise and heroic viceroys of the south, whose resolute stand saved that ancient Empire from anarchy and spoliation." [1]   They also believed Minister Wu ; and their voices, as friends of China, were for the preservation of her integrity and for moderation in every respect. "Hay's achievement," wrote Thayer, "in this Chinese contest gave him an immense prestige.   Throughout the world he was now looked upon as a statesman, honest, disinterested, resourceful and brilliant." [2]   Reference is had to the "open door" correspondence as well as to his conduct during the Boxer uprising; lapse of time confirms fully this effective statement.   The brother Vampires who listened to Hay's brilliant talk when he was forty were not surprised at the development of his parts until he became Secretary of State.   They were prepared for the History, knew that he would be an excellent Ambassador to Great Britain, but were amazed at the able statecraft he displayed in handling Chinese affairs. [3]

---

[1] Addresses, 162.
[2] Life of Hay, ii. 249.
[3] Authorities: Foreign Relations, 1900; Life of Hay, Thayer; Life of McKinley, Olcott; President's Messages of Dec. 1900 and Dec. 1901; Peck.

CHAPTER VI

PRESIDENT making was a concern of the year 1900, which in this case meant practically the action of the Republican Convention that assembled in Philadelphia during June. There was no difference as to the presidential candidate, none as to the platform. According to the prevailing sentiment McKinley had deserved well of the party and the country, and was entitled to another term. The platform was on the point-with-pride order and gloried in the achievements of the Republican party. Merited indeed was all that it said about the Republican opposition to the free coinage of silver and the preservation of the gold standard; for the action of the Republican party had been in line with what believers in sound money advocated. While the platform commended the foreign policy of the President it could not ignore entirely the bloody suppression of the Philippine rebellion which was still on foot, so that the statement regarding the Philippines limped and took no account of patent facts as I have stated them. The platform was adopted with unanimity; there is not "a particle of objection to it," a delegate from New Jersey declared,[1] and he spoke the unanimous voice of the Convention.

The nomination of McKinley and the platform had practically been decided by public opinion freely expressed in various ways in a pre-convention canvass, and traversed Ostrogorski's statement that a National Convention is "a colossal travesty of popular institutions."[2]

---

[1] Official Proceedings of the Repub. Nat. Com. of 1900, 108.   [2] ii. 278.

The Convention and the Republican party were well represented in the words of Theodore Roosevelt, a delegate
at large from New York State, who seconded McKinley's
nomination. "We nominate President McKinley," he
said, "because he stands indeed for honesty at home
and for honor abroad; because he stands for the continuance of the material prosperity which has brought comfort to every home in the Union; and because he stands
for that kind of policy which consists in making performance square with promise." [1]

The whole ticket of 1896 could not be renominated as
Hobart, the Vice-President, had during the year previous
passed away. A new candidate must therefore be chosen
and the convention is remarkable for its choice. The
services of Theodore Roosevelt during the Spanish-
American War made him Governor of New York State,
where he came into collision with Senator Platt and the
Republican organization who were influenced by "the
big corporation men." [2] Roosevelt desired a renomination for governor by the New York State Convention,
which would be held subsequent to the National Convention in Philadelphia, as the governorship interested
him and he had policies which he desired to perfect and
carry out; and he did not want to be sidetracked as
Vice-President. He positively declined a number of
times to be a candidate for that office. Hanna regarded
Roosevelt as erratic and "unsafe" and was emphatically
opposed to his nomination as Vice-President. The natural antagonism between the two became publicly known
at this Convention. Hanna was for the old order with an

---

[1] Official Proceedings, 119.   [2] Roosevelt, Autobiography, 110.

important modification, Roosevelt for the new. And
President McKinley in an unobtrusive way let it be
known that he did not want Roosevelt as a running mate.
Roosevelt arrived in Philadelphia on Saturday, June 16,
and next day had an interview with Hanna, in which he
said frankly to the Senator, "I am not a candidate for
Vice-President and I don't want the nomination. What
I want is to be Governor of New York." [1] Roosevelt's
own account of the matter may be set down as true history : "Senator Hanna appeared on the surface to have
control of the Convention.   He was anxious that I should
not be nominated as Vice-President.   Senator Platt was
anxious that I should be nominated as Vice-President
in order to get me out of the New York Governorship. . . .
My supporters in New York State did not wish me nominated for Vice-President because they wished me to continue as Governor ; but in every other State all the people
who admired me were bound that I should be nominated
as Vice-President." [2]   A supplement to this is a telephone
despatch to President McKinley which reached him late
on Sunday evening, June 17 : "The Roosevelt boom is
let loose and it has swept everything.   It starts with the
support of Pennsylvania and New York practically solid
and with California and Colorado back of it also.   The
feeling is that the thing is going pell-mell like a tidal
wave." [3]

On this Sunday Hanna and Roosevelt failed to reckon
the strength of popular sentiment.   Roosevelt, on ac-

---

[1] Olcott, ii. 275.   [2] Autobiography, 332.
[3] Olcott, ii. 271.   In the midst of the excitement Mrs. Robinson, who
had hastened to Philadelphia at Roosevelt's request, found him in his hotel
room reading the "History of Josephus."   My Brother, T. Roosevelt,
Mrs. Robinson, 196.

count of his course during the Spanish-American War
and the governorship of New York was one of the most
popular men in the country especially in the West, of
the inhabitants of which he was fond. He could not
ignore the manifestation in his favor and was forced to
bow to the will of the people thus expressed. McKinley
also arrived at the same opinion by the Tuesday and thus
telephoned: "The President's close friends must not
undertake to commit the Administration to any candidate. It has no candidate. The convention must make
the nomination; the Administration would not if it could.
The President's close friends should be satisfied with his
unanimous nomination and not interfere with the vice-
presidential nomination. The Administration wants the
choice of the convention and the President's friends must
not dictate to the convention." [1] As soon as Hanna
knew of the President's wishes, he abandoned his opposition and favored unanimity. This was effected on
Thursday, June 21; Roosevelt received on the ballot
taken the vote of every delegate except his own. [2]

The Democratic Convention was held in Kansas City
on July 4. Bryan had made so gallant a fight four years
previously that no one else was talked of for presidential
candidate. He had the nomination for the asking and
he purposed dictating the policy of his party. His article
in the *North American Review* for June showed what
was passing in his mind. "The issue presented in the
campaign of 1900," he wrote, "is the issue between plutoc-

---

[1] Olcott, ii. 279.
[2] Besides the Life of McKinley and Roosevelt's Autobiography I have
used freely the Life of Hanna by Croly, and the Official Proceedings. I
have also consulted *The Nation, passim;* the Life of Foraker, ii.; Platt's
Autobiography, chap. xix.

racy and democracy.   All the questions under discussion
will, in their last analysis, disclose the conflict between
the dollar and the man."   Later on he came to details.
"To-day," he wrote, "three questions contest for primacy
— the money question, the trust question and imperialism." [1]   In placing the money question to the fore, Bryan
displayed greater consistency than wisdom, but as he
had made the contest of 1896 on the remonetization of
silver on the basis of 16 : 1, he was determined that the
question should not now be ignored.   He dominated
the committee on resolutions and the Convention in Kansas City.   They therefore demanded the "free and unlimited coinage of silver . . . at the present legal ratio
of 16 : 1 without waiting for the aid or consent of any other
nation"; but in an earlier resolution they declared that
"the burning issue of imperialism" was the paramount
one of the campaign.

On the first ballot Bryan was unanimously nominated
for President and at Indianapolis on August 8 accepted
the nomination in what he regarded "as one of the most
if not the most important of his political speeches."   The
speech in the authorized volume "revised and arranged
by himself" is entitled "Imperialism" and is mainly
devoted to the Republican management of the Philippines.

The Philippine Islands were acquired as the result of
the Treaty with Spain and it was a well-known fact that
the Treaty could not have been ratified without Democratic votes.   This is tersely stated by Senator Hoar in
his Autobiography.   "Seventeen of the followers of Mr.

---

[1] Pp. 753, 758.

Bryan voted for the Treaty.[1] The Treaty would have been defeated, not only lacking the needful two-thirds but by a majority of the Senate but for the votes of Democrats and Populists. Mr. Bryan in the height of the contest came to Washington for the express purpose of urging upon his followers that it was best to support the Treaty, end the war, and let the question of what should be done with our conquest be settled in the coming campaign."[2] In his speech on "Imperialism," Bryan acknowledged the truth of this statement, defended his position in a careful argument, and then addressed himself to the question, What should we do with the Philippines? He and the Democratic party say, treat the Filipinos as we have promised to treat the Cubans. Why ought not the Filipinos "of right to be free and independent" as well as the Cubans? Admiral Dewey reported that the Filipinos were more capable of self-government than the Cubans, and Bryan stated plainly his purpose. "If elected," he said, "I will convene Congress in extraordinary session as soon as inaugurated and recommend an immediate declaration of the nation's purpose, first, to establish a stable form of government in the Philippine Islands, just as we are now establishing a stable form of government in Cuba; second, to give independence to the Filipinos as we have promised to give independence to the Cubans; third, to protect the Filipinos from outside interference while they work out their destiny just as we have protected the republics of Central and South America, and are, by the Monroe Doctrine pledged to

---

[1] Ten of these were Democrats.
[2] ii. 322. This has been briefly stated in chap. v.

protect Cuba." [1]   Bryan enforced his argument by a poetical citation :

> "Would we tread in the paths of tyranny,
>   Nor reckon the tyrant's cost?
>   Who taketh another's liberty
>   His freedom is also lost.
>   Would we win as the strong have ever won,
>   Make ready to pay the debt,
>   For the God who reigned over Babylon
>   Is the God who is reigning yet." [2]

The important printed contributions to the campaign are this speech of Bryan's and McKinley's letter of acceptance of September 8; of this two-thirds are devoted to the Philippines and a defence of his management.   The letter is in effect a reply to the speech and on the whole may be deemed an effective answer.   The majority of voters probably thought so, although the quotable portions of McKinley's speech of July 12 may have had the greater influence.   We have fulfilled the pledges we made in 1896, he declared, "We have prosperity at home and prestige abroad," yet by the action of the Democratic party, "the menace of 16:1 still hangs over us.   The Philippines are ours and American authority must be supreme throughout the archipelago. . . .   There must be no scuttle policy."   "No blow has been struck except for liberty and humanity and none will be."   The Republican party "broke the shackles of 4,000,000 slaves" and now it has liberated 10,000,000 "from the yoke of imperialism." [3]   Kipling's words represent McKinley's action:

---

[1] Speeches, ii. 46.

[2] In a courteous letter to D. M. Matteson, William J. Bryan says the citation was from a poem written by James A. Edgerton.

[3] Official Proceedings, pp. 148, 149, 150.

"Take up the White Man's burden . . . .'
. . . .
By open speech and simple
An hundred times made plain,
To seek another's profit,
And work another's gain."

The decisive jury was the thirteen and a half million voters. The logical result of Democratic policy was to turn over the Philippines to Aguinaldo and his associates, and there were many who thought as did Senator Lodge, the permanent chairman of the Republican convention, that Aguinaldo was "a self-seeking adventurer and usurper." While the bloody suppression of the Philippine rebellion militated against Republican success, there seemed no other way out. Even if we had an undesirable acquisition, it was ours and our authority must be preserved.

McKinley and Hay, who took an eager though impersonal [1] view of the contest, were solicitous that Hanna should continue as chairman of the Republican National Committee and, when he decided to do so, the President wrote to him: "I am delighted that you have accepted the chairmanship of the National Committee. It is a great task and will be to you a great sacrifice." [2] As we see it now, the election of McKinley appeared a foregone conclusion, but during the canvass there was anxiety among the knowing ones. On September 25 Hay wrote to Henry Adams: "Hanna has been crying wolf all summer, and he has been much derided for his fears, but now everybody shares them. Bryan comes out a frank anarchist again in his letter of acceptance; and Mitchell

---

[1] See letter to Samuel Mather, Life by Thayer, ii. 254.   [2] Croly, 319.

with his coal strike has thrown at least a hundred thousand votes to him." [1] The anthracite coal strike disturbed Hanna and he used his influence with the coal operators to get it settled before election. [2]

Hanna was unquestionably the chief man on the Republican side. All of his executive ability and his knack at raising money were exercised in behalf of his candidate and party. So far, it was 1896 over again, but he had learned to make effective speeches on the stump and, as he was much in demand from the several committees, he appeared before many audiences throughout the country. The burden of his talk was that Republican success and administration had given prosperity to the manufacturer, merchant and financier, and the full dinner pail to the laborer. His more effective work was through his personality. Westerners beyond Ohio had the idea that he was a "bloated millionaire," and when they came to see a man of easy bearing, of democratic ways, placing himself on a par with the common man and hear his rough speech adapted to their easy comprehension, they were converted to the Hanna cult. "This trip," wrote Croly with singular penetration, "helped to make Mr. Hanna personally popular throughout the West, just as his first stumping tour in Ohio had made him personally popular in his own State. As soon as he became known, the virulence and malignity with which he had been abused reacted in his favor. When he appeared on the platform, the crowd, instead of seeing a monster, found him to be just the kind of man whom Americans best understand

---

[1] Letters Privately Printed, iii. 196.
[2] Croly, 328; *The Nation*, Nov. 1, 1900, 342.

and most heartily like. He was not separated from them by differences of standards and tastes or by any intellectual or professional sophistication. The roughness of much of his public speaking and its lack of form which makes it comparatively poor reading, were an essential part of its actual success. He stamped himself on his speeches just as he had stamped himself upon his business. His audiences had to pass judgment on the man more than on the message and the man could not but look good to them." [1]

"I have never wondered," said Senator Dolliver of Iowa, "as so many have, that Hanna suddenly developed into a great orator. . . . I was present in 1900 at the stock yards in Chicago when I had a glimpse of the colossal personality of this man which made a very profound impression on my mind. We took him down there to speak to the working people of Chicago, and curiously enough — a very strange anomaly under institutions like ours — a large part of the audience had assembled there, not to listen to him but to prevent him from speaking; and with noise, riot, tumult, disturbance, and breach of peace . . . that surging multitude for one hour and thirty minutes fought an unequal battle with the genius of a single man; and at 10 o'clock, the audience calmed, controlled, fascinated, he began one of the most remarkable political speeches it was ever my good fortune to hear." [2]

Next in importance was Roosevelt's stumping. If we may judge his speeches by his letter of acceptance, he defended Republican policy and administration. He insisted that the remonetization of silver meant disaster,

---

[1] P. 340.   [2] Address, April 7, 1904.

and that our acquisition of new provinces was in the line
of national development; it meant expansion and not
"imperialism or militarism." [1]   He added strength to the
ticket and his appearance and manner increased his strong
personal popularity. "His attitude as speaker," wrote
Thayer, "his gestures, the way in which his pent-up
thoughts seemed almost to strangle him before he could
utter them, his smile showing the white rows of teeth,
his fist clenched as if to strike an invisible adversary,
the sudden dropping of his voice, and levelling of his fore-
finger as he became almost conversational in tone, and
seemed to address special individuals in the crowd before
him, the strokes of sarcasm, stern and cutting, and the
swift flashes of humor which set the great multitude in
a roar, became in that summer and autumn familiar to
millions of his countrymen; and the cartoonists made
his features and gestures familiar to many other millions." [2]

As was the case four years previously, Bryan was in-
defatigable on the stump. By his and the Democratic
criticism of the Republican management of the Philippines, he gained the support of the anti-Imperialists, at
the head of whom was Carl Schurz, but as *The Nation*
remarked on another occasion, "Those who sup with the
devil, even with a long spoon, are sure to have to swallow
a nauseous portion at the end." [3]   Bryan had the cordial
support of Tammany Hall and showed his appreciation
of it when he came to New York, declaring "Great is
Tammany! And Croker is its prophet." This disgusted
Carl Schurz, who wrote, "Bah! Wasn't it awful!" [4]

---

[1] Official Proceedings, 180.
[2] Roosevelt, 151.   [3] June 28, 1900.
[4] Reminiscences, iii. 447.

Despite the strength of the cause and the candidates, there will be hours of depression among those destined to victory. While 1900 must be put down as a year of prosperity, there were weeks when business halted owing partly to a reaction from the flush times of 1899, partly to the depression usual in a presidential year and partly to a real alarm by financiers at the prospect of Bryan's success. His policy was distrusted and his administrative power feared. This feeling is well reflected in John Hay's private letter of October 31: "This last week of the campaign is getting on everybody's nerves. There is a vague uneasiness among Republicans, which there is nothing in the elaborate canvasses of the Committee to account for. I do not believe defeat to be possible, though it is evident that this last month of Bryan, roaring out his desperate appeals to hate and envy, is having its effect on the dangerous classes."[1] Also Hay wrote to Henry Adams on the same day, "Our folks are curiously nervous about next Tuesday. The canvass is all right — the betting also. But nobody knows what Jack Cade may do."[2]

Forty-five States voted on November 6, giving McKinley 292 electoral votes to Bryan's 155, and a plurality in the popular vote of 849,000, — the greatest Republican victory since 1872.[3] Bryan carried only four Northern States, Colorado, Idaho, Montana and Nevada; as compared with 1896 he lost his own State of Nebraska, Kansas, Utah, Washington, South Dakota and Wyoming.

---

[1] To Samuel Mather, Life of Hay, Thayer, ii. 256.
[2] Letters Privately Printed, iii. 201.
[3] Grant in 1872 had a greater percentage of the popular vote. In 1896 Kentucky gave McKinley 12 of her 13 votes. All went to Bryan in 1900.

Hanna and Roosevelt undoubtedly contributed to the result west of the Missouri River.

By McKinley's reëlection in 1900, wrote Croly, "The Republicans had received a clear mandate to govern the country in the interest of business expansion." [1] J. Pierpont Morgan, with his great reputation of railroad reorganizer as well as banker, now turned his attention to the iron and steel business, where it was thought his faculties would have full play. Under the régime of competition, men bid against one another for trade. Pig iron manufacturers were eager for the custom of the steel mills, who in turn sought to sell to the railroads. Confining our attention to the period from the close of the Civil War to 1900, fluctuations had been great. A glut of pig iron naturally induced low prices, a large capacity for the manufacture of steel resulted in the enterprising managers bidding against one another for whatever trade was in sight. Fostered by the "hard times" following the panic of 1873, long-headed men developed the manufacture of "specialties" in steel, but every pound so made took the place of the same quantity of iron with the result that mills devoted exclusively to iron could not in dull periods make the two ends meet. Failures came and the list of bankruptcies in the iron trade was appalling. It was always a "feast or a famine" was a common expression and the hard years were followed by the "Benner boom" of 1879 when prices went beyond all reason. This, with less violent fluctuations after 1881, was the history of the iron trade to the panic of 1893. Requiring large capital and managing ability, the number of steel

---

[1] Life of Hanna, 341.

mills was not large, but the feeling among them was not harmonious unless the common dislike of all the others for Andrew Carnegie and his methods might draw them together in sympathy. Between 1893 and 1900 a process of consolidation had been going on so that a large part of the steel business of the country had become centred in seven concerns outside of the Carnegie Steel Company. The consolidation was effected by promoters and "water" was a component part of all of the common and preferred stocks which made up the capitalization. The rebound from the panic of 1893 made easy the flotation of these securities and in some of the concerns Morgan had an interest. The question arose after the election outcome of 1900, Could not these seven be united into one concern? and with one accord it seemed to be agreed that Morgan was the man to finance the enterprise. Attracted to it, he went to work and soon had under way the combination of the seven, which would have been a huge concern with the Carnegie Steel Company its chief opponent.[1]

Andrew Carnegie came from Scotland to America as a poor boy and got a job in a cotton mill in Allegheny City at the wage of $1.20 per week. He told of his experience: "For a lad of twelve to rise and breakfast every morning, except the blessed Sunday morning, and go into the streets and find his way to the factory and begin to work while it was still dark outside and not be released until after darkness came again in the evening, forty minutes

---

[1] A convenient list of these seven plus the Carnegie Steel Co., the American Bridge Co., and the Lake Superior Consolidated Iron Mines is given by Cotter, 22. See likewise Berglund, 102. "The American Bridge Co., and the Lake Superior Consolidated Iron Mines entered the Steel Corporation soon after its organization."

only being allowed at noon, was a terrible task." [1]   At
fourteen he became a messenger boy in a telegraph office,
attracted the attention of Thomas A. Scott who asked
him to be his "clerk and operator."   Scott took a fancy
to Carnegie and suggested investments, so that he developed into what his boy friends termed a "capitalist."
When Scott became Vice-President of the Pennsylvania
Railroad, Carnegie became superintendent of the Pittsburg division and remained for a number of years in the
service of this great company.   Prospering in his investments he organized the Keystone Bridge Works, which
was among the first, if not the first, to construct successful iron bridges. [2]   Thus, becoming a business man, working on his own account, he resigned his position on the
Pennsylvania Railroad, and devoted his attention first
to the making of pig iron and then by a natural development to the manufacture of steel.   Financial vicissitudes,
differences with partners, manufacturing difficulties had
to be overcome, but in 1900 he was the greatest steel-
maker in the world and could produce steel rails cheaper
than anywhere else on earth.   His history has been told
in an unsympathetic yet truthful way by J. H. Bridge,
who had been private secretary of Herbert Spencer and
literary assistant to Carnegie himself; yet from a careful
reading of this book one cannot be otherwise than convinced that, in this day of material progress, Carnegie
was a great man.

Carnegie's faults were those of many self-made men
and lay on the surface.   He was egotistical and con-

---

[1] The Gospel of Wealth, x.   "The hours hung heavily upon me and in
the work itself I took no pleasure." — Carnegie's Autobiography, 34.
[2] See Carnegie's Autobiography, 115, 122.

ceited and had an opinion dogmatically expressed on
many subjects on which confessed ignorance would have
been better. Apparently without reverence for those
who had made study the pursuit of a lifetime, he took
issue with Greek scholars on the desirability of a study
of Greek; and there was scarcely a subject in English
or American politics as to which he had not a positive
opinion. Dispensing a generous hospitality from his
Scotch retreat of Skibo Castle he was much run after
for contributions to all sort of enterprises. This phase
of his life is well represented in a contemporary cartoon.[1]
Was it not humiliating, said an observer, "to see people
in a London drawing-room cringing before him in order
to get a cheque?" But it was no better in the United
States, where he was besieged by all sorts of men
for money contributions to their favorite enterprises.
"With sincerity," said Confucius, "unite a desire for
self-culture." Carnegie was sincere. "The man who
dies rich, dies disgraced," he wrote in 1899.[2] He was not
then rolling in superabundant wealth, but when he possessed it after the event I am about to relate he carried
out his dictum of years before. That he had a desire
for self-culture is evident from his reading of books which
he displayed in his writings and from his benefactions.
When he was a working-boy in Pittsburg he had constant recourse to a free library, and he told of his "intense longing" for a new book. "I resolved," he wrote,
"that if ever wealth came to me, it should be used to
establish free libraries." [3] The Anglo-Saxon world knows
how well this resolution was carried out.

---

[1] Cleveland *Plain Dealer; Cosmopolitan Mag.*, Sept. 1901.
[2] The Gospel of Wealth, 19.   [3] Ibid., 28.

Such was Andrew Carnegie, the poor boy, the great manufacturer of steel and after 1901 the possessor of two hundred and fifty millions. Of course he was helped by the high tariff and he took advantage of all the conditions in the country that he had made his own.

Men may poke fun at him because he wrote, "I sympathize with the rich man's boy and congratulate the poor man's boy," for most of the "immortals" have been born to "the precious heritage of poverty," [1] but it was the sincere observation of a poor boy, who during his life had amassed millions.

We now return to the organization of the United States Steel Corporation in which were displayed some of Morgan's best and doubtful qualities. He was keen enough to see that the Carnegie Steel Company must be in the combination and while Carnegie was desirous of selling, the Scotchman was determined to get a good price. His policy of threat was effectually used. According to Bridge, he wrought through a "press agent" and by newspaper interviews. It was given out that owing to a disagreement with the Pennsylvania Railroad he would give all possible business to the railroad running from Pittsburg to Conneaut, the Lake Erie terminus, and would also take advantage of the cheap water transportation. Striking thus directly at the Pennsylvania Railroad, he also threatened to build at Conneaut the largest

---

[1] The Gospel of Wealth, xii. In his Autobiography, 31, Carnegie gave a charming picture of the life of his family after they had left Scotland and settled in Allegheny City and then wrote: "The children of honest poverty have the most precious of all advantages over those of wealth. The mother, nurse, cook, governess, teacher, saint, all in one; the father, exemplar, guide, counsellor and friend! Thus were my brother and I brought up. What has the child of millionaire or nobleman that counts compared to such a heritage?"

and best equipped tube works in the country, giving a
direct blow to Morgan who was largely interested in the
National Tube Company, one of the combining concerns.
It was likewise well known that the Carnegie Steel Company could make steel cheaper than any other company
in the world. Carnegie had his price which Morgan, with
apparently little hesitation, paid. It was said at the time
that the canny Scotchman had outwitted the New England Yankee. Thus the so-called "billion dollar trust"
was launched. It consisted of 550 million common stock,
550 million preferred, and 304 million [1] 5 per cent bonds;
all of the bonds went to the Carnegie Steel Company
of which Andrew Carnegie got the lion's share. The
Carnegie Steel Company also received $98,277,120 in
preferred stock and $90,279,040 in common stock at par.
Reckoning the bonds of $303,450,000 worth one hundred
cents on the dollar, the preferred stock at 82 and the
common stock at 38, the Carnegie Steel Company received $418,343,273 for their property. It was no won-
der then that Andrew Carnegie was counted worth $250,-
000,000.

The other combining companies [2] took stock. Of the
1,100,000,000 stock all of the common and some of the
preferred was "water"; but as there was an abundance
of "water" in the combining companies, the increase
of stock and the increase of "water" do not seem to have
been objected to. For their services the Morgan syndicate received 649,897 shares of the common stock of the

---

[1] Probably $303,450,000. There were also about 56 million of bonds
owned by the combining companies which the U. S. Steel Corporation
assumed. Berglund, 71.
[2] See again Cotter, 22; Berglund, 102.

United States Steel Corporation and an equal number
of the preferred. At $38 a share for the common
and $82 a share for the preferred, this amounted to
$77,987,640. This was all effected on a cash capital of
25 millions, which the syndicate received back, plus 200
per cent in dividends.[1] Although J. P. Morgan himself
never speculated in the way of buying or selling stocks
on a margin, he comprehended the stock market well
and engaged a celebrated manipulator to market the
shares, which were put upon the market as paying dividends of four per cent on the common and seven per
cent on the preferred. Starting on the curb at 38 for
"steel common" and 82¾ for "steel preferred," these
stocks were soon admitted on the Stock Exchange and
within a month advanced to 55 and 101⅞ respectively,
although perhaps considerable of this advance was due
merely to "matching of orders." [2]

It was popularly supposed that the United States Steel
Corporation possessed about two-thirds of the Lake Superior iron ore and Connellsville coal of the country, although the actual figures of production do not substan-
tiate the popular belief. In the four years, 1902–1905
inclusive, the United States Steel Corporation shipped
56 per cent of the Lake Superior ore, produced 36 per
cent of the Connellsville coke, 70 per cent of Bessemer
steel ingots, 60 per cent of Bessemer steel rails and 51 per
cent of open hearth steel ingots and castings. There was
naturally some efficiency in operation by bringing so many
plants under one head and management, and there was

---

[1] American Finance, Noyes, 300; Life of Morgan, Hovey, 216.
[2] Noyes, 300.

a praiseworthy effort to get workingmen, superintendents and other employés interested in the Company by selling them shares at lucrative rates.   The United States Steel Corporation constantly stabilized prices.   After its formation there was no violent enhancement of values during a time of "boom," no "runaway market" in steel. On the other hand, during times of depression, prices never went below what would give a fair profit.

The distribution of interests by Jupiter does not work in our common world and did not under Morgan.   In short, the United States Steel Corporation was too big for effective work.   As Morgan discovered, it is exceedingly difficult to find a man of sufficient ability and character to head so large a concern.   His first efforts were failures and while the present [1] "chief executive officer," Judge Elbert H. Gary, is a decided success, it is doubtful whether his successor will possess his eminent qualities. But at no time has the United States Steel Corporation made steel absolutely or comparatively as cheap as did the Carnegie Steel Company just before the combination was made.   Carnegie said that "his partners knew nothing about making stocks and bonds but only the making of steel." [2]   The difference lies in the combination of companies and the adjustment of interests with a sharpened pencil on a writing pad in a Wall Street office and presence at the works among the men where steel is turned out.   Charles M. Schwab, the first President of the United States Steel Corporation, in New York

---

[1] 1920.

[2] Trusts of To-Day, Montague, 37.   "America is soon to change from being the dearest steel manufacturing country to the cheapest." — Written before the sale to J. P. Morgan.   Autobiography of Andrew Carnegie, 227.

City and Europe, was a different Schwab from him who, in the grime and dirt of Pittsburg, administered the affairs of the Carnegie Steel Company. "Schwab had graduated at Braddock under Captain Jones and, displaying exceptional ability as a manager of men, had quickly won his way from one of the lowest positions in the yards to the highest in the office. His cheery friendliness made him especially popular among the workmen." [1] Anyone who knew personally William R. Jones, or as he was familiarly called, Captain Bill Jones, and what he stood for, may well join in this tribute which Bridge paid him: "Greater than all of Jones's inventions was his progressive policy. . . . The young men whom he trained ably seconded him. . . . The famous scrap heap for outgrown, not outworn, machinery was instituted by Jones, who never hesitated to throw away a tool that had cost half a million if a better one became available. And as his own inventions saved the company a fortune every year, he was given a free hand. Under this greatest of all the captains of the American steel industry [Jones] a group of younger men grew up, trained in his broad views and habituated to his progressive methods; so that when in 1889 he was killed in a horribly tragic way by the explosion of one of his furnaces, there were men ready trained to take up his work and continue it." [2] Carnegie said that he owed his success to Jones and to Schwab; [3] and

---

[1] Bridge, 245. Schwab wrote, July 24, 1919, on his photograph which is reproduced in Carnegie's Autobiography opposite 256: "To my dearest friend and 'Master' with the sincere love of 'His Boy.'"

[2] Bridge, 105.

[3] Cotter, 89. "Jones," so wrote Andrew Carnegie in his Autobiography, "bore traces of his Welsh descent. . . . He came to us a two-dollar-

he once suggested for his epitaph, "Here lies the man who knew how to get around him men who were cleverer than himself." [1]   He said, "The nation that makes the cheapest steel has the other nations at its feet." [2]   Hendrick also affirmed that Carnegie did not like "this Wall Street coterie." [3]   What a pity that, with his desire to get out of business, such inducements were offered that he must perforce go in with them!   For the United States Steel Corporation has never been the asset for the country that the Carnegie Steel Company was or might have been.   Carnegie in the United States was greater than Krupp in Germany.   The one made the implements of peace; the other was skilful in the production of necessaries of war.   Carnegie had a fit successor in Henry Clay Frick to carry on his work while he might have devoted himself to his noble benefactions.   Unfortunately however, the two had quarrelled.

While the Carnegie foibles are apparent, he was ahead of his age in his devotion to "gentle Peace."   How much he thought of it, why the world ought to have it, why

---

a-day mechanic from the neighboring works at Johnstown. . . . He had volunteered as a private during The Civil War and carried himself so finely that he became captain of a company which was never known to flinch.   Much of the success of the Edgar Thomson Works belongs to this man."   In later years, Carnegie offered him an interest which would have made him a millionaire without entailing any financial responsibility.   This Jones declined saying, "No, I don't want to have my thoughts running on business.   I have enough trouble looking after these works.   Just give me a big salary if you think I am worth it."   "All right, Captain, the salary of the President of the United States is yours." "That's the talk," rejoined Jones.   P. 203.

"Captain Jones described me as having been born with two rows of teeth and holes punched for more, so insatiable was my appetite for new works and increased production." — Ibid., 112.

[1] The Age of Big Business, B. J. Hendrick, 68.
[2] The Age of Big Business, Hendrick, 60.   [3] P. 81.

war was the worst of evils, are amply testified to in his writings, private letters, expressed desires and by his benefactions. No wonder then that the great war of 1914 broke his heart.[1]

Different from Carnegie, J. P. Morgan had inherited wealth and a good education; he possessed the confidence of the investing public. It was thought in 1901 and 1902 that he could accomplish anything. Ex-Mayor Grace's experience was that of many. One morning he received a brief letter by post saying that he had been awarded a hundred thousand dollar share in the Underwriting syndicate of the United States Steel Corporation. Having had no conversation with Morgan on the subject, knowing only by hearsay of the organization of the "billion dollar" trust, he sent his cheque for what was asked for, being $8000, from his entire confidence in the banker. Although liable up to the amount of $100,000 he never got a further call for more but in due time received back the money he had sent and his share of the enormous profits of the Underwriting. "I never made money as easy as that," he said.[2]

The organization of the "billion dollar steel trust," as the Steel Corporation was called, the impetus of McKinley's second election, the rebound from the panic of 1893, the war of 1898 and the stock depression of 1899 turned men's heads in 1901. Stocks went up, money was easily made, thoughts ran in hundred millions, men and women were extravagant, champagne corks popped, the assertion was made that the day of panics had passed

---

[1] Preface to Carnegie's Autobiography by Mrs. Carnegie, v.
[2] Life of Morgan, Hovey, 216.

and all went as merry as a marriage bell. "The out-
burst of speculation during April 1901," wrote Noyes,
"was something rarely paralleled in the history of speculative manias." Men who were made millionaires by
their sales of United States Steel Corporation shares became speculators in Wall Street. "The 'outside public'
meantime seemed to lose all restraint. A stream of ex-
cited customers of every description brought their money
to New York and spent their days in offices near the Stock
Exchange. . . . The newspapers were full of stories of
hotel waiters, clerks in business offices, even doorkeepers
and dressmakers, who had won considerable fortunes in
their speculations." [1] Happily this booming condition
was for a time brought to an end by a quarrel between
Edward H. Harriman on one side and Morgan and James
J. Hill on the other. Both parties desired control of the
Northern Pacific Railroad and began bidding against
one another for its possession. The stock ran up from
160 to 1000 but "all other stocks broke violently" and
a good part of Wall Street was for two hours on that day
of May 9, 1901, "technically insolvent." [2] Those who
term this a real panic and are fond of historical parallels
may refer to 1881 and point to the facts that the Indian
corn crop in 1901 was with two exceptions [3] the smallest
in twenty years and that a President was also assassi-
nated. The strife for the Northern Pacific was a battle
of financial giants but all this turmoil would have been
avoided had they composed their differences before instead of after this Wall Street shock.

---

[1] Noyes, 301.

[2] Noyes, 306.   [3] 1881, 1894.   In

1900	the crop was	2,105,000,000
1901	the crop was	1,522,000,000
1902	the crop was	2,523,000,000

Elated with his success in the Steel combination Morgan attempted a similar enterprise in connection with transport across the Atlantic Ocean. He got hold of the Dominion Line, the American and Red Star, the Atlantic Transport Company, the White Star Line and the Leyland, paying for the ships more than they were worth. The chairman of the Leyland Company told the shareholders that Morgan's offer was so high "that no management had a right to refuse it." [1]　Morgan attempted to get hold of the German lines and the Cunard Company but these for similar reasons would not sell their ships.

As I have previously written, the whole amount of cash in the flotation of the United States Steel Corporation was twenty-five millions; the rest was faith in Morgan. It may be readily conceded that he alone in the country could effect such an organization but, was it worth while to abuse that faith and put upon the market at a supposedly valuable price more than 550 millions of "water"? True, Morgan's friends argued that the capitalization was based upon earnings and not upon the value of the property; but what consolation was that to "widows and orphans" who had invested in Steel Common at from 38 to 55 because it paid four per cent, when the Corporation suspended dividends on the Common and the stock went below 10 as it did in 1903? The decline in the market was from 101 for the Preferred down to 49, and from 55 for the Common to 10.　No wonder that Morgan was depressed coming as it did with the utter failure of his ship combine.　Morgan has "fallen down" in his steamship combination, was a usual remark.

This depression in 1903 was called "the rich men's

---

[1] Noyes, 303.

panic." After what is known as the Northern Pacific
Railroad corner, speculation again grew rampant as the
"bumper wheat crop" in 1901 made up for the shortage
of corn, but early in 1903 it became apparent that the old
rules of business and finance remained in force and the
"little panic" between two economic crises occurred. As
Morgan said in a newspaper interview it was a case of
"undigested securities." [1]

The Boston *Herald* of January 10, 1920, commented on
"The Greatest Epic in the History of Big Business" by
which it meant the Standard Oil Company, that is typi-
fied by John D. Rockefeller. In the constituent companies which made up the United States Steel Corporation one finds the "Lake Superior Consolidated Iron
Mines," which is put down as the "Rockefeller interests"
and which was necessary to the Corporation as owning
a large quantity of Lake Superior iron ore. Lake Superior ore had become the basis of the steel industry from
its quantity and, while the Bessemer process ruled, from
so much of it being low in phosphorus. Ores high in
phosphorus were inadmissible as that element was at
enmity with steel. The "Rockefeller interests" were
not absorbed until after the Carnegie Steel Company.
The transaction is simply related by Rockefeller. "After
some negotiation," he wrote, "Morgan made an offer
which we accepted whereby the whole plant — mines,
ships, railways, etc. — should become a part of the United

---

[1] Noyes, 308. Besides works already referred to, I have used in this
account, Trusts of To-Day, G. H. Montague; Commercial and Financial
Chronicle, 1900, 1901; *The Nation*, 1900, 1901; Articles of Gleed, Mac-
chen, Ely, *Cosmopolitan Mag.*, 1901; article of R. S. Baker, *McClure's
Mag.*, Nov. 1901; Peck; Life of Hill, Pyle, ii.

States Steel Corporation. The price paid was, we felt, very moderate considering the present and prospective value of the property." [1]

John D. Rockefeller was one of the directors of the huge corporation and he is comprehensible to us from a study of Napoleon I and from a remark made by Herbert Spencer in 1882 when he was considered a great philosopher, "Practically business has been substituted for war as the purpose of existence." [2] From a bookkeeper Rockefeller had become a partner in a small commission house on the Cuyahoga River in Cleveland, when the discovery of petroleum in Western Pennsylvania started many men in Cleveland, bent on making their fortunes, in that direction. Nothing like the excitement had been known since the discovery of gold in California.[3] Samuel Andrews had invented an easy and cheap process of cleansing the crude oil with sulphuric acid and oil refineries went up in Cleveland as if by magic. Rockefeller, like Cassius, was not fat and thought much and he made up his mind that for him success lay in oil; he embarked on its manufacture, made a copartnership with Andrews and H. M. Flagler and the three went into the business as did many others. For a while the demand for "the light of the world" could not be supplied but eventually the supply became greater than the demand and Cleveland manufacturers were confronted with the fact that the refining of oil in Cleveland for the whole trade of the

---

[1] Random Reminiscences, 131.

[2] After-dinner speech in New York, Nov. 9, 1882. Essays, iii. 484.

[3] An animated account of the discovery of oil and the excitement ensuing is given by Oberholtzer in his History of the United States, i. 250 et seq.

world was a geographical absurdity, as the bulk of the
trade lay east of the oil regions. The Cleveland re-
finers were engaged in a cutthroat policy; they bid
against one another in the purchase of the crude oil from
Pennsylvania, and in the other direction were intense
competitors for the sale of the refined.   In 1870 the Standard Oil Company was formed with Rockefeller as the
directing agent, who conceived the idea of uniting all
under one head by the purchase of all of the Cleveland
refineries.   This he did, paying a fair price and giving
the owners the choice of Standard stock or cash for their
works. Those who took cash thought that they were
getting a bargain; those who took stock became rich.

Rockefeller had difficulty in raising money to meet
his desires as the financial "bigwigs" of Cleveland, with
two exceptions, were opposed to his scheme and thought
that he was taking too many and too great chances.   At
this time he would have preferred to pay for the refineries
that he was buying in stock rather than in money, as the
one commodity was more plenty than the other.   "We
invariably," he wrote, "offered those who wanted to sell
the option of taking cash or stock in the company.   We
very much preferred to have them take the stock because
a dollar in those days looked as large as a cart-wheel, but
as a matter of business policy we found it desirable to
offer them the option and, in most cases, they were even
precipitate in their choice of the cash.   They knew what
a dollar would buy but they were very skeptical in regard
to the possibilities of resurrecting the oil business and
giving any permanent value to these shares." [1]   The tale

---

[1] Random Reminiscences, 95.

of Rockefeller's financial anxieties seems strange to the younger generation which associates him with unlimited amounts of money, but those whose memory goes back to the time know how true is his account and that he does not exaggerate in any way his difficulties. "We had our troubles and setbacks," he wrote, "we suffered from severe fires; and the supply of crude oil was most uncertain. . . . At best it was a speculative trade and I wonder that we managed to pull through so often." [1]

The Standard Oil Company was thus launched.[2] If Rockefeller did not say it, he thought that, "The coal oil business belongs to us."[3] Keeping in mind the similarity and the difference between war and trade how like Napoleon's expression in 1811, "Three years more and I am lord of the universe!"[4] With great method and untiring zeal Rockefeller wrought for the control of the manufacture and business of refined oil. He acted in accordance with the conditions of his time. After the panic of 1873 railroad business became poor and the railroads were "cutting one another's throats" for whatever business was in sight. Rockefeller took in the situation and, by his control of a large amount of desirable freight, compelled rebates not only on his own shipments but on those of his competitors.

William H. Vanderbilt, who succeeded his father in the control of the New York Central and Lake Shore Railways, important lines of communication for the oil

---

[1] Random Reminiscences, 83.

[2] I do not digress into a history of the South Improvement Company, believing that it died in embryo. See Wealth against Commonwealth, Henry D. Lloyd, 59.

[3] History of the Standard Oil Company, Tarbell, ii. 34.

[4] Sloane's Napoleon, ii. 235.

business, was then supposed to be the richest man in the country, worth $200,000,000. Only one man in the world, the Duke of Westminster, had an equal amount, but his return from this capital was not as great as Vanderbilt's. His appreciation of the ability shown in the management of this enterprise is therefore important. Vanderbilt testified in 1879: "These men [the Standard Oil Company managers] are smarter than I am a great deal. They are very enterprising and smart men. I never came in contact with any class of men so smart and able as they are in their business." [1]

Rockefeller's handling of the railroads placed him in a commanding position. Herbert Spencer said in the speech already quoted, "I hear that a great trader among you deliberately endeavored to crush out everyone whose business competed with his own." [2] This was unquestionably Rockefeller's method but he was absolutely fair to all of his stockholders and gentle to competing refineries who would work with him on his own terms, which in every case turned out advantageously for those manufacturers. The crude oil producers looked upon him "with superstitious awe," so Miss Tarbell wrote. "Their notion of him was very like that which the English common people had for Napoleon in the first part of the nineteenth century . . . a dread power, cruel, omniscient, always ready to spring." [3] He undoubtedly squeezed the crude oil producers as he did recalcitrant partners of friends whom he started in outside operations. It was owing to these tactics that the man who from nothing

---

[1] Tarbell, The History of the Standard Oil Company, ii. 252.
[2] Essays, iii. 484.
[3] Tarbell, The History of the Standard Oil Company, ii. 63.

had made a billion, had to be guarded by detectives. He could have no such funeral as Peter Cooper had, of which a journalist at the time said Jay Gould, a rich man of the day, with all of his money, could not buy such a funeral.

Rockefeller accepted the conditions of the game and played it accordingly. The management of the Standard was one of efficiency in every direction. "It seemed absolutely necessary," Rockefeller wrote, "to extend the market for oil by exporting to foreign countries which required a long and most difficult development." [1] This was in exact keeping with the ideas of the day and expressed a thought in many minds. Rockefeller put the idea in active operation, and, while making money for the Standard made it an important factor in the country's foreign trade. [2] When the "spellbinders" declaimed that the tariff was the mother of all trusts, the Standard Oil Company must be excepted, as its operations were not dependent on the tariff legislation of Congress.

In line with efficiency, every bit of waste was carefully looked after. His scientific men were encouraged in the development of by-products which were sold cheaply, brought comfort to many households and swelled the foreign exports. Rockefeller himself was a remarkable judge of men and gathered around him a number of able lieutenants who wrought loyally under his direction. While he himself was a puritan in life he never made his personal system of morality a guide in the choice of those

---

[1] Random Reminiscences, 82.

[2] Exports fiscal years 1870–71 to 1899–1900 in value, Corn $1,073,333,-598, Wheat $2,495,182,543, Wheat Flour $1,382,075,300, Cotton $6,409,-112,711, Refined Mineral Oil $1,294,953,816.

under him. Was the man equal to his job? seemed to
be the sole test. For efficient coöperation the United
States never saw the equal of the Standard.

Rockefeller was the first to develop on a large scale
the sale of a natural product direct from the producer
to the consumer. He suppressed the middleman and
of course made enemies. A man who had a small broker-
age business dependent upon the Standard, on which
he supported in economic ease a small family, could
not refrain from exclaiming, when deprived of his means
of living, as he thought of the work of this powerful rich
man, "He has taken from me my one ewe lamb." To
such considerations Rockefeller was callous. Mercy in
business never entered into his calculations. Not unlikely
he ascribed talk, critical of his work, to envy, which he
illustrated in his Reminiscences with the action of an
Irish neighbor who built an extremely ugly house, the
bright colors of which were offensive, as he looked out
from his windows; therefore he moved some large trees
to shut out the house from his view. Why are those
large trees moved? the Irishman was asked, to which
came the quick reply, "It's invy, they can't stand looking
at the evidence of me prosperity." [1]

Rockefeller quoted the expression of an old and experienced Boston merchant, "I am opposed on principle
to the whole system of rebates and drawbacks — unless
I am in it." [2] This was undoubtedly the opinion
of business men until this practice was forbidden by the
Interstate Commerce Law of 1887. But before 1887 the
Standard had developed its system and, as it increased

---

[1] Random Reminiscences, 72.   [2] Ibid., 112.

in power and wealth, dictated to those high in command
of the railroads, getting low rates which enabled it to
crush competitors, or when that was unnecessary, to
amass hitherto unheard of wealth.

As Rockefeller's operations were successful he had no
difficulty in obtaining all of the money that he desired,
so that we see in the Standard a corporation efficiently
directed with a real genius at its head and an ever ready
supply of cash. To develop the foreign trade and to
supply the East it was soon seen that the crude oil must
be refined at the seaboard, hence refineries were established at Brooklyn, Bayonne in New Jersey, Philadelphia
and Baltimore. Having made dictatorial arrangements
with the railroads, organized trade with Europe, Asia,
Africa, the East and West of his own country, a common
man would have rested on his oars satisfied with his great
accomplishments. Not so Rockefeller who was ever on
the watch. Pipe-lines had early been in operation to
gather the oil from the wells to the railroads, of which
the Standard had its share, but in 1879 it was demonstrated by an opposition company that crude oil could
be pumped over the mountains and so reach the seaboard.
Pipe-line transportation was much cheaper than railroad
even if the railroads cut down their carrying charges to
cost. Under this new competition all of Rockefeller's
carefully made contracts with the railroads, so far as the
carrying of crude oil was concerned, were for naught,
but he was equal to the emergency. Within five years
he owned all of the pipe-lines to the seaboard or had them
under his control. With great effect he wrote in his book:
"The entire oil business is dependent upon the pipe-line.
Without it every well would be less valuable and every

market at home and abroad would be more difficult to serve or retain." [1]

Constantly in litigation the Standard employed the best lawyers to fight its cases. Its policy ever to get hold of the ablest was in this particular exemplified with good results.

Did the Standard make the light of the world cheaper? An affirmative answer is at once given by its apologists, a negative by its critics. For ourselves we shall do well to accept the judgment of the intelligent historian of the Standard Oil Company, Gilbert H. Montague, who with the energy of youth investigated fully the matter. "The vexed question," he wrote, "of the effect of the Standard Oil combination on the price of refined oil will probably never be settled." [2] It certainly stabilized prices. Under Cleveland competition, as it existed before 1871, there would have been an era of low prices succeeded by one of high, in entire accordance with the law of supply and demand. Under Standard management the price could not have been excessive or it would have lacked candid defenders. On the other hand there were the large dividends and the fact that everyone connected with the Standard grew rich.

Henry D. Lloyd in "Wealth against Commonwealth" makes a sharp criticism of the Standard Oil Company, and his remedy for the evils it and other trusts caused is State Socialism. This discussion will go on as long as socialists and individualists exist. But the student of men and affairs cannot overlook that "government is

---

[1] Random Reminiscences, 84.
[2] The Rise and Progress of the Standard Oil Company, 136.

some of us, and those not the best of us, put over the rest of us." [1]   After a careful reading of this book of Lloyd's one inclined to individualism cannot fail to approve the statement of the reviewer of *The Nation*, "Were we not satisfied from evidence *aliunde*," it said, "that the managers of the Standard Oil Company had violated both law and justice in their attempts to suppress competition, we should be inclined to acquit them after reading this screed. It is quite beyond belief that these men should be capable of the height and depth of wickedness attributed to them, even if they possessed the superhuman powers with which they are credited. It is plain upon Mr. Lloyd's showing that their competitors would be no better than they if they had similar opportunities and it is impossible to arouse sympathy for men whose complaint is that they were not allowed to make enormous profits, for it appears to have been the policy of the Standard Company to buy out its rivals at reasonable rates." [2]

Miss Tarbell, from a number of articles in *McClure's Magazine*, devoted to muckraking, has written two volumes entitled "The History of the Standard Oil Company" in which her industrious research can do no other than compel admiration from anyone who seeks historic truth. Her examination of documents that bear upon the subject seems thorough and no one can attempt a consideration of the Standard without recourse to the many facts that she has uncovered. All the same, the feeling grows that she had determined on her thesis and in her book had sought facts which should support her preconceived impressions. Again must one have recourse to *The*

---

[1] Cited from memory but the remark was, I think, made by Professor W. G. Sumner.   [2] *The Nation*, Nov. 8, 1894, 348.

Nation. "The writer" [*i.e.* Miss Tarbell], it said, "has either a vague conception of the nature of proof or she is willing to blacken the character of John D. Rockefeller by insinuation and detraction." But he "has been caught in no worse crimes than underselling his competitors and getting rebates from railroads. . . . It is matter of public notoriety that Mr. Rockefeller is offensively reticent. . . . In impassioned . . . language a desperate struggle is described between the powers of evil incarnate in the Standard Oil Company and the powers of goodness appearing in a metaphysical entity called the 'Oil Region.' This being, it appears, loved virtue for its own sake; it believed in independence and fair play; it hated the rebates and secret rates; it hated, but it also feared, its adversary. . . . The 'Oil Region' means a number of men engaged in the wildest kind of speculation, many of whom proved themselves willing to engage in every kind of wickedness of which the Standard Oil Company was accused." It "might say like the French deputy to his constituents, 'So intense was the corruption that even I did not altogether escape.'" [1]

A careful consideration of the subject, with a thorough reading of Lloyd's and Miss Tarbell's books cannot fail to impress an inquirer with the great ability shown by Rockefeller, who was to business what Napoleon was to war and to civic society. In Rockefeller may be seen a ripe development of the application of energy to resources. This quiet, reticent man, thinking and listening, as he stropped his penknife over the heel of his boot, like the traditional Yankee whittling a stick, made combinations which startled the world. Always given to

---

[1] *The Nation*, Jan. 5, 1905, 15.

reflection when not taking needed physical exercise, reading no book but "Ben Hur,"[1] he moved men upon his chess-board like pawns in the game.   Sincerely religious, it must have been a surprise to him that his methods were questioned when he simply played the game as he found its conditions, and supposed that he never violated the tenets of the Christian religion as commonly understood.   Outside of religion and physical exercise he pursued one single idea and was eminently successful from the grasp of his mind.

The question must arise, Is it well for the State to have such huge fortunes as those of Rockefeller and Carnegie accumulated in a lifetime?   It must be said in their defence that they accomplished the difficult art of giving, that their benefactions were noble and that they set a pattern for other rich men, whose gifts and bequests have been on the side of civilization.   In the amassing of such wealth it is well that they or their descendants did not spend it in luxurious or riotous living; that they themselves obeyed the call of duty and were as systematic and wise in their dispensations as in their acquirements. That their gifts made for the good of civilization, however, will fail to convince the mass of voters, who cannot see that fine pictures, well-collected libraries, endowed universities, cure of disease and prophylactic treatment compensate them for a deprivation of their share of the cake in favor of Rockefeller, Carnegie and others.[2]

---

[1] Up to 1918.   The Bible of course excepted.

[2] For authorities not specifically referred to I have consulted Industrial Commission Reports, vol. i. 19.   House docs., 1899–1900, vol. 93; 1901–1902, vol. 82;   Trusts of To-Day, Montague; Noyes, Forty Years of American Finance;   Burton J. Hendrick, Age of Big Business; Peck; *The Nation*, 1900, 1901.

McKinley's second inaugural address (March 4, 1901)
was a pæan to the successful accomplishment of the past
four years. Then there was a deficit, now a surplus;
then depression, now activity. "The national verdict
of 1896," he declared, "has for the most part been exe-
cuted." His personal bearing, action and amiability had
contributed much to the achievement of what he stated
in fitting words : " Sectionalism has disappeared. Division
on public questions can no longer be traced by the war
maps of 1861." [1] "I can no longer be called the President of a party," he said to his Secretary; "I am now the
President of the whole people." [2]

Between the second inauguration and his death
McKinley enjoyed his office and the hold which he had
on the people; his content was marred by the alarming
illness of his wife during a trip to the Pacific coast. On
his return to Washington, he was obliged, because of her
condition, to decline an invitation to the Commencement of Harvard University and receive the honorary
degree of Doctor of Laws. In answer to repeated public
requests that he should again be a candidate for the presidency, he made an open statement that under no circumstances would he accept a nomination for a third
term.

He had promised to visit the Buffalo fair, believing,
as he there said, "Expositions are the timekeepers of
progress. They record the world's advancement." " The
crowning and original feature of this Exposition,"
wrote Robert Grant, was the illumination by the electric

---

[1] Messages and Papers, Supplement, 163.
[2] Life of McKinley, Olcott, ii. 296.

lights; the power for the electricity was furnished by Niagara Falls. "The time fixed for the ceremony of illumination," continued Grant, "is half-past eight, just as the summer twilight is deepening into darkness. . . . There is a deep silence and all eyes are riveted on the electric tower. Suddenly . . . we have a veritable fairyland; the triumph not of Aladdin's lamp but of the masters of modern science over the nature-god, Electricity."[1] Dooley likewise visited the fair. "They tell me," he wrote, "that at th' Pan-American show in th' city iv Buffalo th' ilicthric light is made be Niag'ra Falls. . . . Hogan seen it, an' he says it makes th' moon look like a dark lanthern. They speak iv th' sun in Buffalo th' way a motorman on a trolley line wud shpeak iv a horse car. 'Th' sun is settin' earlier,' says he to Conners, th' thruckman that wus towin' him. 'Since th' fair begun,' says Conners, 'it hasn't showed after eight o'clock. We 'seldom hear iv it nowadays. We set our clocks be th' 'risin' an' settin' iv th' lights.'"[2]

The President's visit to the Buffalo fair was delayed until September when, during a crowded reception, he was shot by an anarchist (September 6) who, in the line of approaching people, pretending to have an injured hand, concealed, in the handkerchief wrapped around it, a revolver from which two shots dealt the death-blow to the President. The fatal shot was fired on a Friday afternoon. McKinley lingered for over a week and at times strong hopes were entertained for his recovery, but these were vain, and early on Saturday morning, September 14, he passed away.

---

[1] *Cosmopolitan Magazine*, Sept. 1901, 453.
[2] *Cosmopolitan Magazine*, Sept. 1901, 478.

The crowd, amazed at the attempt on the life of their beloved President, threatened to lynch the assassin but McKinley, stricken to death, showed his respect for the law in his words, "Don't let them hurt him." [1]   Then his thoughts dwelt upon his wife, who, accompanying him to Buffalo, was at a neighboring house. "My wife — be careful, Cortelyou, how you tell her — oh, be careful!" A week later when he and all of his friends knew that the end was near, he said, "It is God's way. His will, not ours, be done"; then he repeated some lines of his favorite hymn, "Nearer, my God, to Thee." [2]   Involuntarily came to many lips, "See how a Christian can die." The journalist who had sneered at "the pious McKinley" could not, from his skeptical view, appreciate the depth and sincerity of McKinley's religious nature.

Roosevelt, on hearing of the assassination, hurried to Buffalo but, on the assurance that the President would recover, left for the Adirondacks whence he was hastily summoned again. Before his arrival McKinley had passed away and, when reaching Buffalo, Roosevelt was met by a request from Secretary Elihu Root, the ranking member of the Cabinet who was there, that he "take the constitutional oath of President of the United States." To this he replied: "I shall take the oath at once in accordance with your request, and in this hour of deep and terrible national bereavement I wish to state that it shall be my aim to continue absolutely unbroken the policy of President McKinley for the peace and prosperity and honor of our beloved country." [3]

[1] For the trial and execution of McKinley's assassin, see my vol. viii. 151.

[2] Life of McKinley, Olcott, ch. xxxiv.

[3] Messages and Papers, Supplement, 298.

Elihu Root, McKinley's Secretary of War, said: "I have talked with him [McKinley] again and again before a Cabinet meeting and found that his ideas were fixed and his mind firmly made up. He would then present the subject to the Cabinet in such a way as not to express his own decision, but yet bring about an agreement exactly along the lines of his own original ideas, while the members often thought the ideas were theirs. . . . He cared nothing about the credit but McKinley *always had his way.* . . . He had vast influence with Congress. He led them by the power of affectionate esteem not by fear. He never bullied Congress." [1] Shelby M. Cullom, Senator from Illinois for thirty years, wrote: "We have never had a President who had more influence with Congress than McKinley. . . . I have never heard of even the slightest friction between him and the party leaders in Senate and House. . . . He looked and acted the ideal President. He was always thoroughly self-poised and deliberate; nothing ever seemed to excite him and he always maintained a proper dignity." [2] President Roosevelt said in his first Message to Congress: "At the time of President McKinley's death he was the most widely loved man in all the United States; while we have never had any public man of his position who has been so wholly free from the bitter animosities incident to public life. . . . To a standard of lofty integrity in public life he united the tender affections and home virtues which are all-important in the make-up of national character." [3]

From my point of view it will ever be a regret that the

---

[1] Olcott, ii. 346.   [2] Fifty Years, **275.**
[3] Messages and Papers, Supplement, 315.

long-standing distrust of and enmity to Spain should have come to a head during McKinley's administration. For he was essentially a peace minister. Coming before the public, the high-priest of protection, he had, through the exercise of executive authority, modified his views. He was diligent in the enforcement of the reciprocity provision of the Dingley Act and named John A. Kasson to negotiate in accordance therewith reciprocity agreements. It was not necessary that these agreements should be ratified by the Senate but some Senators, who were more strongly high tariff than McKinley himself, thought that France had gotten the better of Kasson in the bargain.[1] Nor was McKinley's recommendation of free trade with Puerto Rico immediately adopted. In his message of December, 1899, he said, "Our plain duty is to abolish all customs tariffs between the United States and Puerto Rico and give her products free access to our markets." It took him a little over a year and a half to accomplish this but he had the satisfaction before his death of seeing complete free trade with the island.[2] In the speech that he made in Buffalo the day before his assassination, he showed how far behind him he had left the doctrines of ultra-protection. "A system," he said, "which provides a mutual exchange of commodities, is manifestly essential to the continued and healthful growth of our export trade.

---

[1] Kasson made the agreement with France on May 28, 1898; it was proclaimed on May 30. He made an agreement with Italy on Feb. 8, 1900; it was proclaimed on July 18, 1900; another with Portugal on May 22, 1899; it was proclaimed on July 12, 1900.

There were later made the following agreements, but not by Kasson: Germany, proclaimed July 13, 1900. Switzerland, proclaimed Jan. 1, 1906. Spain, signed Aug. 1, 1906. Bulgaria, proclaimed Sept. 15, 1906. Great Britain, proclaimed Dec. 5, 1907. Netherlands, proclaimed Aug. 12, 1908.

[2] Willoughby, Territories and Dependencies, 113.

We must not repose in fancied security that we can forever sell everything and buy little or nothing. If such a thing were possible, it would not be best for us or for those with whom we deal. We should take from our customers such of their products as we can use without harm to our industries and labor. . . . The period of exclusiveness is past. The expansion of our trade and commerce is the pressing problem. Commercial wars are unprofitable. A policy of good will and friendly trade relations will prevent reprisals. Reciprocity treaties are in harmony with the spirit of the times, measures of retaliation are not." "We find our long-time principles echoed," declared *The Nation*, "to our unfeigned satisfaction." [1]

McKinley, however, did not live up to the expectations of the Civil Service reformers, inferred from his expressions and attitude when a member of the House. The testimony of William D. Foulke of Indiana is of high value. Singularly in favor of Civil Service reform, on excellent terms with Eaton, Curtis, Schurz, Dana and others who labored in the vineyard, he supported by speech and action McKinley in 1896 and 1900 and was a level-headed man who could look on both sides of any question. By his order of July 27, 1897, asserted Foulke, McKinley "greatly strengthened the competitive service"; it provided that no removal should be made "except for just cause." In his Annual Message of December, 1897, he said that the merit system "has the approval of the people and it will be my endeavor to uphold and extend it," and in the ensuing session of Congress "he opposed all efforts to repeal or change the law. But in

---

[1] Sept. 12, 1901, 197.

the administration of it," continued Foulke, "the executive department showed great weakness." An anticipated and forecasted order was promulgated on May 29, 1899, which marked "the first considerable reduction in the area of the merit system since the Civil Service law was enacted in 1883." As a quasi-atonement he extended the merit system to the Philippine Islands "by his instructions to the Philippine Commission in April, 1900." "As the campaign of 1900 drew near," Foulke went on to say, "the opinions of Civil Service reformers were divided." The anti-imperialists, among whom was Carl Schurz, "felt a deep resentment at the backslidings of McKinley and could see nothing of his extension of the competitive system to the Philippines which could atone for breaking his promises regarding that system in the United States." [1]

McKinley's action in regard to Civil Service reform was tortuous. He seemed swayed by opposing forces. Undoubtedly the one opposed to Civil Service reform was represented by Mark Hanna who sincerely believed that, for the good of the country and the party, he himself, the heads of the departments, the senators and representatives could make better appointments than could be secured by any system of competitive examination.[2]

---

[1] W. D. Foulke, Fighting the Spoilsman, 119, 122, 123, 125. See Richard H. Dana's review, *Amer. Polit. Science Rev.*, Feb. 1920.

[2] Authorities not specifically mentioned. Proceedings of National Civil Service Reform League, 1900, 1901; Carl Schurz, Speeches, Correspondence, etc., vi.; Foraker, Notes of a Busy Life, ii.; *The Nation, passim.*

CHAPTER VII

WITH our new colonies it has been impossible to preserve a chronological unity of narrative. It is now necessary to enter upon an account of Puerto Rico, Cuba and the Philippines, going back to a point beyond which the narrative has already taken us and terminating ahead of the time to which the history of our domestic transactions will be carried.

Puerto Rico may be easily disposed of. In the words of Archibald C. Coolidge, its annexation, "being a natural consequence of the Spanish War, met with little opposition from any quarter." Writing in 1908 he sums up with, "All told, the record of American rule has been satisfactory and creditable."[1] This is supported by the words of a competent and intelligent English authority, Eustace Percy, who wrote about 1919, "In Porto Rico the United States has pursued a most liberal and progressive policy."[2] To Joseph B. Foraker, chairman of the Senate Committee on Puerto Rico, fell the duty of drafting the organic act which determined our relations with Puerto Rico. This became a law in 1900, is known as the Foraker Act, was upheld somewhat over a year later as constitutional by the United States Supreme Court, and is thus referred to with commendable pride by the author, "The mere fact that this law has continued in force, practically without change, ever since it was

---

[1] The United States as a World Power, 143, 145.
[2] The Responsibilities of the League, 87.

enacted, now full fifteen years ago, is enough to indicate that it proved satisfactory when put into practical operation." [1] "This Act," wrote William F. Willoughby, "is in every respect an important document. It may be said to stand to our new insular possessions in much the same relation as the Northwest Ordinance did to our dependent territory on the mainland." Willoughby was Treasurer of Puerto Rico from 1901 to 1907 and, while in that office, wrote a book in which he gave an excellent account and analysis of the Foraker Act summing up with, "The problem that Congress had to meet when it framed the organic act — that of providing a system of government that should at once grant a maximum of local autonomy and at the same time make provision for sufficient central control — was an exceedingly difficult one. If it has erred, it has been in immediately granting too much rather than too little." [2]

"Whatever may be the fate of Cuba in the future," wrote Archibald C. Coolidge, "the treatment she has received at the hands of the United States in the decade since she was made free will remain something to be proud of." [3] The pledge contained in the Teller Amendment was faithfully kept. After the Treaty of Paris the government of Cuba was for a while under the direction of the American Army. Elihu Root had become Secretary of War and he was insistent that Cubans be prepared for a civil government to be administered by themselves.

---

[1] Notes of a Busy Life, Foraker, ii. 82. This was published in February, 1916. The statute is printed in U. S. Statutes at large, 56th Cong., vol. 31, p. 77.

[2] Territories and Dependencies of the United States, 83, 117.

[3] The United States as a World Power, 130.

But before the American Army left, a great work was accomplished in sanitation — "the marvel of the age," Latané terms it.[1] "Read the story of yellow fever in Havana and Brazil," wrote Dr. William Osler, "if you wish to get an idea of the powers of experimental medicine; there is nothing to match it in the history of human achievement."[2] The work in Cuba is well stated by Secretary Root in his report of November 27, 1901. "The eastern part of the island," he wrote, "is entirely free from yellow fever. The western part is practically free there being but a few cases in or about Habana. This dreaded disease has passed from one of the leading causes of death to one of the least frequent. The reduction of death rate in Habana alone, as compared with the former death rate, shows an average of approximately 3700 lives per year saved, and Habana has changed its position from one of the most unhealthy cities to one of the most healthy. The control of yellow fever, acting upon the results of investigation as to its causes, prosecuted under the direction of the military government, appears to be now practically absolute."[3]

The chief credit is of course due to General Wood without whose command nothing could be done, but associated with him in this "extraordinary service in ridding the island of yellow fever" were Major Walter Reed and Major William C. Gorgas. "The name of Dr. Jesse W. Lazear, contract surgeon," continued Secretary Root, "who voluntarily permitted himself to be inoculated with the yellow fever germ, in order to furnish a necessary

---

[1] The United States as a World Power, 182.
[2] "Man's Redemption of Man," in *American Mag.*, Dec., 1910, 251.
[3] Report, House Docs., 57th Cong. 1st Sess., 39.

experimental test in the course of the investigation, and
who died of the disease, should be written in the list of
the martyrs who have died in the cause of humanity." [1]

A census was taken showing a population of 1,572,797,
of whom 34 per cent were able to read and write, while
66 per cent were illiterate.   The desire and need of popular education were great and both private and public
efforts were made in this direction.   The wise President
of Harvard University, Charles W. Eliot, was to the fore,
raised a fund for the purpose and invited a number of
Cuban teachers to the summer school in Cambridge where
they could learn from masters of the art how to instruct
others eager for education but ignorant of the way to get
it.   These teachers, 1281 in number, spent the summer
in attending the school and in a study of neighboring
institutions of art and practical manufacture, and, before
they went home, were given a free visit to New York
City and Washington. [2]

All the while, progress was making toward the training
of the people of Cuba for self-government.   A basis of
suffrage was agreed upon [3] and on June 16, 1900, municipal officers throughout the entire island were elected.   As
soon as the new municipal governments were fairly in-
stalled, a call for a constitutional convention was made,
and thirty-one delegates to it were orderly chosen.   The
convention met in Havana on November 5, 1900, and was
opened by General Wood.   But before Cuba could be
let go, the relations between the island and the United
States must be defined.   This was done in the Platt

---

[1] Report of Dec. 1, 1902.   House Docs. 57, Cong. 2d Sess., 10.
[2] Military and Colonial Policy, Root, 198.
[3] For restrictions on universal suffrage, ibid., 194.

Amendment to the Army Appropriation Bill which became a law on March 2, 1901. The author of this was Orville H. Platt of Connecticut who is fitly described by his biographer, Louis A. Coolidge, as "an old-fashioned senator," and the biography is said to be "the story of a life unselfishly devoted to the public service." He feared that he could not pass the measure independently through the Senate at the short session and so had recourse to a rider to an appropriation bill.

The Platt Amendment provided that:

I. The independence of Cuba should not in any way be impaired by any compact with a foreign power.

II. A proper limitation was made as to the amount of any public debt that Cuba should contract.

III. Cuba consented to the intervention of the United States "for the preservation of Cuban independence, the maintenance of a government adequate for the protection of life, property and individual liberty and for discharging the obligations imposed by the Treaty of Paris on the United States."

IV. The acts of the United States during the military occupancy should be validated.

V. Cuba would maintain "and as far as necessary" extend the work of sanitation.

VI. The Isle of Pines should be omitted "from the proposed constitutional boundaries of Cuba."

VII. Cuba was to furnish the United States "lands necessary for coaling or naval stations." [1]

Article III caused the greatest amount of opposition in the Cuban constitutional convention and this was

---

[1] See America as a World Power, Latané, Hart's American Nation Series, 189.

finally quieted by a statement of Senator Platt and an official communication to a committee of the convention by the Secretary of War.[1] Then the provisions of the Platt Amendment were appended to the Cuban Constitution.

Like many important documents the authorship of these wise provisions has been in dispute. The editors of the series of the Root publications have maintained that it was drafted by Secretary Root and this claim was made indeed during the lifetime of Senator Platt. The true genesis of the Platt Amendment, however, is truthfully and effectively told by Senator Platt in a private letter of January 1, 1904: "The original draft was my own. . . . It was changed from time to time, somewhat in language but not in spirit, in consultation both with Republicans of the Committee, President McKinley and Secretary Root. A final consultation between myself and Senator Spooner put the document in its complete form."[2] Root's titles to greatness were so many that he would be the last man to claim aught that was not fully his own, while Senator Platt's admiration at an early day for Root was unbounded. He, said the Senator, is discharging the duties of Secretary of War better than any other man could. But he could fill any position in the Cabinet and indeed he might serve as President with capacity and wisdom.

"At any rate," wrote the Senator in a private letter, "the United States will always, under the so-called Platt Amendment, be in a position to straighten out things if they get seriously bad."[3]

---

[1] Life of Platt, Coolidge, 344; Military and Colonial Policy, Root, 214.
[2] Life of Platt, Coolidge, 351, *et ante;* Military and Colonial Policy, Root, viii.   [3] Life of Platt, Coolidge, 349.

Elections were held in Cuba under the Constitution on the last day of December, 1901, when governors of provinces, members of the House of Representatives and presidential and senatorial electors were chosen; these electors met during the following February and elected a President, Vice-President and senators. The civil government of Cuba was duly inaugurated and the American troops withdrawn on May 20, 1902. With pardonable pride Elihu Root wrote as Secretary of War in his report of 1902: "I know of no chapter in American history more satisfactory than that which will record the conduct of the military government of Cuba. The credit for it is due, first of all, to General Leonard Wood." In his order of July 4, 1902, Root said that the officers and enlisted men "have with sincere kindness helped the Cuban people to take all the successive steps necessary to the establishment of their own constitutional government; . . . they have governed Cuba wisely, regarding justice and respecting individual liberty; have honestly collected and expended for the best interests of the Cuban people the revenues" of the island.[1]

The peace, the health, the independence of Cuba are necessary to the United States. A commercial arrangement should be made with her under which she can live, said Root in his report of November 27, 1901.[2] This meant that in a reciprocal arrangement the duties on her sugar and tobacco should be reduced. This proved to be a long and tedious process owing to the opposition of some selfishly protected interests, but the arrangement was finally submitted to both Houses of Congress.

---

[1] Report of Dec. 1, 1902, 9, 14.   [2] P. 53.

Through the influence of President Roosevelt and the work of Senator Orville H. Platt (to mention some of the agencies working to this end) a treaty of reciprocity between Cuba and the United States was ratified late in 1903. During the contest Senator Platt wrote in a private letter: "The reduction on Cuban imports will not hurt the sugar or tobacco industry one particle. Neither the sugar trust nor the tobacco trust will derive the slightest benefit from it. The talk about it has been the greatest exhibition of expansive bosh that I have ever known." [1]

By the Platt Amendment it was provided that a treaty between the two countries should embody its provisions. This was made. Our course towards Cuba is well summed up by Theodore Roosevelt: "We made the promise to give Cuba independence; and we kept the promise. . . . We also by treaty gave the Cubans substantial advantages in our markets. Then we left the island, turning the government over to its own people." [2]

The Philippines is a knotty question. It has been a political issue and the course of the administration has aroused sentimental objection. The literature on the subject is enormous and observers, who have remained long and have written candid accounts, have arrived at opposite conclusions. [3] It is best, therefore, in the maze

---

[1] Life of Platt, Coolidge, 381.

[2] Autobiography, 545. In this study of Cuba I have been much helped by Latané's "America as a World Power." See the Chapter in Life of Platt on "Cuban Scandals and Allowances."

[3] Charles B. Elliott wrote: "Many writers, American and English, who have favored the public with their views on the Philippines . . . sug-

of contradictions to rely on the man, who, more than any other one, is responsible for our policy — Elihu Root. It will be told later how he came into administrative office. For the moment it suffices to say that he regarded the United States as the greatest of his clients, and that an ambassador of the Russian Czar said that having met most of the public men of Europe, he knew no one who was as able as Elihu Root.

Before he called Root to his aid President McKinley had inaugurated the government of the Philippines. His message to Otis, who was the military commander in the islands, stated the mission of the United States but in it he said that we had succeeded to the "sovereignty of Spain" and that our aim was "benevolent assimilation." Now McKinley was entirely sincere and the anti-Imperialists, who afterwards played upon those words, failed to comprehend the depth of his religious nature. The overpowering feeling which swayed him was religious and this cannot be better stated than in the private letter to him of Senator Orville H. Platt of August 15, 1898. "I feel that I ought to say," he wrote, "that during the past week I have been well over the State of Connecticut and I am satisfied that nine-tenths of the people of the State have an intense feeling that we should insist upon the cession of all the Philippine Islands. These who be-

---

gest Kipling's famous 'Pagett M. P.' who visited India in winter and 'spoke of the heat of India as the Asia solar myth.' " As his entertainer returned homeward he wrote :

> "And I laughed as I drove from the station but
>   the mirth died out on my lips
> As I thought of the fools like Pagett who write
>   of their Eastern Trips."

The Philippines to the End of the Commission Government, 376.

lieve in Providence see, or think they see, that God has placed upon this government the solemn duty of providing for the people of these islands, a government based upon the principle of liberty, no matter how many difficulties the problem may present. They feel that it is our duty to attempt its solution. Among Christian thoughtful people the sentiment is akin to that which has maintained the missionary work of the last century in foreign lands. I assure you that it is difficult to over-estimate the strength and intensity of this sentiment. If, in the negotiations for peace, Spain is permitted to retain any portion of the Philippines it will be regarded as a failure on the part of this nation to discharge the greatest moral obligation which could be conceived." [1]

Connecticut is a small State but it has great influence especially in the Western States through which President McKinley made his "famous Western journey" and had his own opinion confirmed. The attempt of many anti-Imperialists to hint that love of gain was the prime cause of our taking the Philippines is not borne out by the record.

The first interference by Congress with the Commission government was by the Spooner Amendment to the Army Appropriation Bill, which was approved on March 2, 1901; this was decidedly opposed to any attempt to exploit the islands.[2] The Philippine Commission, in their report to the Secretary of War of November 1, 1902, spoke of "the burdensome restrictions upon the investment of

---

[1] Life of Platt, Coolidge, 287.
[2] The Spooner Amendment is printed in Root, Milit. and Colonial Policy, 255. See speech of Senator Lodge on an earlier bill. Speeches and Addresses, 317.

capital in lands and mines in these islands. . . . The requirements," they continued, "that no corporation shall own more than 2500 acres, stops absolutely the investment of new capital in the sugar industry and in the tobacco industry. It takes away any hope of bringing prosperity to these islands by the extending of the acreage in the cultivation of these two important products of the archipelago. It very much interferes with the investment of capital in railroad enterprises, because they are naturally connected with the possibilities of transportation of sugar and tobacco from the interior to the seaports." [1] In their report of December 23, 1903, they returned to the subject and recommended that "the limitation ought either to be removed entirely or be increased so as to allow the acquisition of at least 25,000 acres of land." [2]

The charge that our acquisition was "a greedy land-grabbing game" may have come from the open plans of promoters of new enterprises. So far as I have been able to discover there were no extravagant profits except those made out of the 70,000 American soldiers by some half dozen "American trading companies," who acquired "quick and large profits" referred to by Civil Governor William H. Taft in his report of November 15, 1903.[3] It was the old story of Pistol,

> "I shall sutler be
> Unto the Camp and profits will accrue." [4]

While on this subject the idea may at once be dismissed that the United States made any money out of the Philippines. Archibald C. Coolidge, whose authority can-

---

[1] Report, 7.   [2] Report, 9.
[3] P. 49.   [4] King Henry V., act ii., scene 1.

not be gainsaid, wrote in 1908: "American capital has not come in in the way that was expected, partly on account of the legislation passed to protect the natives against exploitation, but more particularly because people have found it safer and more profitable to invest their money nearer home." [1] It is true that the manipulation of the tariff, although a concession was made to the products of the Philippine Islands, was not enlightened policy. Governor Taft desired absolute free trade with the islands but it took a number of years, and then under his own presidency (1909), to effect this consummation.

President McKinley was a conscientious Methodist, and he fully believed that in the Philippines the white man's burden was laid upon the United States. As men act from mingled motives, the idea of personal fame doubtless was bound up in his action. He was a student of American history and knew it well for the years that came within his personal remembrance. Every American President since 1865 has emulated the fame of Lincoln, as did McKinley, when in his speech accepting the nomination in 1900, he declared: "The Republican Party . . . broke the shackles of 4,000,000 slaves and made them free, and to the party of Lincoln has come another supreme opportunity which it has bravely met in the liberation of 10,000,000 of the human family from the yoke of imperialism." [2] He likewise believed that the possession of the Philippines would be an assistance to our growing trade in the Orient.

No one can write on this subject without devoting a large amount of study to the arguments of the anti-

[1] The United States as a World Power, 170.
[2] Life of McKinley, Olcott. ii. 287. This was then stated

Imperialists with whose statements, so far as they can be tortured into reasoning that we had no business trying to govern people 7000 miles away, I am in entire sympathy. Moorfield Storey's acute logic and large present intelligence would make one almost feel that Charles Sumner was on earth again interpreting the Constitution and the acts of the President by the truths of the Declaration of Independence. His opposition to our work in the Philippines was sincere and was urged by a sacrifice of present ease and earthly honors. For he was of the stuff of which martyrs are made and, in earlier days, would have suffered for his opinions at the stake. Carl Schurz, according to a personal friend, was a revolutionist and thus he showed himself in his opposition to the Philippine policy. His speeches were those of an orator and his well-rounded periods put his position with great force. His argument, which was generally concurred in by the anti-Imperialists that we should treat the Philippines as we had treated Cuba, was well put, attested as it was by the despatch of Admiral Dewey that the Filipinos "are far superior in their intelligence and more capable of self-government than the natives of Cuba, and I am familiar with both races."[1] But Schurz's plan in giving self-government to the Philippines was "to make the Philippine Islands neutral territory as Belgium and Switzerland are in Europe."[2] Schurz fortunately did not live to see the guarantee of Belgium's neutrality treated as a mere "scrap of paper," nor did he become disabused of his profound admiration for the German Emperor, Wilhelm

---

[1] Despatch of Dewey to Sec. of Navy, June 27, 1898.
[2] Speech of Oct. 17, 1899. Speeches, etc., vi. 108.

II. "Whether the Emperor of Germany did not at one time wish to acquire the Philippines, I do not know," he said. "But if we offered him the Philippines to-day with our compliments, he would doubtless ask, 'How large an army do you have to employ to subjugate the country?' The answer would be, 'At present 60,000 men; we may need 100,000.' The Emperor would smilingly reply, 'Thank you. Offer this job to someone who is as foolish as you have been.' He would probably be too polite to say so, but he would doubtless think so." [1] At this time a majority of the best informed people in the United States and England believed that Germany would take these islands if she could get them and apply, if need be, the ruthless methods which the Emperor told his troops to employ in China. "Spare nobody," he said, "make no prisoners, use your weapons in a manner to make every Chinaman for a thousand years to come forego the wish to as much as look askance at a German." [2]

The opposition of Senator George F. Hoar was pathetic. A true Republican, he loved McKinley, who, late in 1898, was committed to taking the Philippines. When he saw the President during December of that year and was taken by the hand with the question, "How are you feeling this winter, Mr. Senator?" "Pretty pugnacious, I confess, Mr. President," "The tears came into his eyes and McKinley said, grasping my hand again, 'I shall always love you whatever you do.'" [3] Hoar planted

---

[1] Speech of Sept. 28, 1900, ibid., 248.
[2] July 2, 1900. The Kaiser's Speeches, Wolf von Schierbrand, 260 (1903).
[3] Autobiography, ii. 315.

himself on the Declaration of Independence that "governments derive their just powers from the consent of the governed." He was a true disciple of Charles Sumner "to whom," he said, "the Declaration of Independence was another gospel." [1] We ought to have treated the Philippines as we did Cuba, he affirmed, and had we done so, a government under Aguinaldo and his associates would have been formed as stable as the governments from the United States to Cape Horn. A democracy, he declared, "cannot rule over vassal states as subject people without bringing in the elements of death into its own constitution." [2] This idea was extensively elaborated by Carl Schurz, but it had great force coming from a true American and a loyal Republican like Senator Hoar.

In truth there is something admirable in these three men pleading for the rights of eight million brown people as they had hitherto for four million blacks. It is the old story of the superior taking the part of the inferior, and it involves the subjugation of race pride and putting one's self in the place of the brown or black man.

McKinley had aspirations after culture and was especially fond of college men. He decided to send a Commission to the Philippines, at whose head should be Jacob G. Schurman, President of Cornell University. During January, 1899, Schurman was summoned to Washington and such an invitation was extended to him. He demurred first because he feared that he could not leave the University and then he said, "To be plain, Mr. President, I am opposed to your Philippine policy; I never

---

[1] Speech in the Senate, Jan. 9, 1899; see Senator Lodge's argument on "consent of the governed." Speeches and Addresses, 326.

[2] Senate speech.

wanted the Philippine Islands." "Oh," was the reply,
"that need not trouble you; I didn't want the Philippine
Islands either; and in the protocol to the treaty I felt
myself free not to take them, but in the end there was
no alternative." The American people certainly would
not consent to leave the Philippines to Spain, the President argued, and, as that was no longer a question, if
"American sovereignty were not set up, the peace of the
world would be endangered." We, so he implied, certainly owed responsibilities to the world at large. The
President desired this Commission to act as an advisory
Cabinet and he especially wished to know what sort of
political relations it was wise to establish between the
United States and eight million [1] brown men of Asia.
He desired aid in shaping such a policy and at the same
time a tactful coöperation with the naval and military
authorities at Manila.[2] Schurman accepted the Presidency of the Commission and McKinley named as his
associates Admiral Dewey, General Otis (who was the military commander in the Philippines), Charles Denby and
Dean C. Worcester of the University of Michigan.

When Schurman arrived in Manila he found a war in
progress which was an interruption to his peaceful errand.
The American and Philippine armies had faced each other
near Manila for a number of weeks in hostile array. The
Americans had bought the sovereignty of the islands
from Spain but the Filipinos supposed that in the event

---

[1] The first Commission adopted that figure (15). The Census of 1903
made the population somewhat less. Enc. Brit.; Blount, Amer. Occupation of the Philippines, 567. Williams wrote that the population to the
square mile was about 66, to 350 in Java, 290 in Japan, 200 in India. Odyssey of the P. Com., 306.

[2] Schurman, A Retrospect and Outlook, 2.

of American success they were to be granted their independence. The fight which broke out on February 4,
1899, was therefore one between sovereignty and independence. The feeling which became pretty general
among the Filipinos may be stated thus: "If the Americans are going to look on us and treat us as the Spaniards
have done for three hundred years we do not want them
here." [1]   Aguinaldo [2] was the head of the Filipinos and he
was a Malay of marked ability. A born leader he knew
how to consolidate the different factions in the islands.
While he was far from being the "George Washington
of the Orient," as some of the anti-Imperialists in America called him, he probably conducted as well as possible
the war for independence. But it is a question whether
he and most of his followers would have opposed the
Americans had they known that they came there not to
exploit the islands but to assist them in their progress
toward civilization. The Filipinos, however, had been
fed with promises until they had come to distrust the
white man; and the minute blood was shed the sympathy of the mass ran with their brown brothers. The
Filipino soldiers were, however, no match for the Americans, and while they had modern rifles they did not know
how to use them, so that casualties on their side were
large and entirely out of proportion to the losses of the
Americans. By the end of 1899 organized resistance to
the United States Government came to an end, and thereafter the insurrection took the form of guerilla warfare
which, in many cases, degenerated into brigandage. In
November of this year Aguinaldo disappeared into the

---

[1] Unofficial Letters of an Official's Wife, Edith Moses (1908), **74**.
[2] See note at end of chapter.

wilderness and apparently played little or no part in the guerilla warfare.

The Schurman Commission became one of investigation and in their report of January 31, 1900, maintained that the Philippine Islands could not stand alone. To become "self-governing and independent" they needed the "tutelage and protection of the United States." But the "goal of the intelligent Filipinos" was ultimate independence — "independence after an undefined period of American training." [1] "Should our power by any fatality be withdrawn," it said, "the Commission believe that the government of the Philippines would speedily lapse into anarchy, which would excuse, if it did not necessitate, the intervention of other powers and the eventual division of the islands among them." [2]

About ten per cent of the Filipinos were educated men, of high intelligence. They knew Spanish, the civilization and the literature of Spain, but naturally they were not all saints. A goodly proportion of them were office-seekers of the type we know in the United States, and they desired independence in order to hold the purse strings of the nation, while if they were under an American protectorate they would be protected from other Asiatic and European countries by the American Navy, in the event that they should misconduct themselves in foreign affairs. The radicals, whose true leader was Aguinaldo, influenced a majority of this ten per cent and they swayed the mass. All but less than a million were Ro-

---

[1] Report, 83.
[2] Senate hearings on affairs in the Philippine Islands, 2983. Henry Cabot Lodge was the efficient chairman of the committee before whom the hearings were had.

man Catholic Christians and this religion was imposed upon them by the Spanish conquest three hundred years before, and the Spaniards brought to them also Spanish civilization which proved to be an element of great progress. In one respect at least the Filipinos stood high in comparison with other Orientals and even Europeans — in their regard for women. Antedating the Spanish conquest there was an equal inheritance law. Never were soldiers and officers of the American Army more mistaken than when they called the Filipinos "niggers," as in all essentials the Filipinos stood far in advance of the American negro.[1] Really the Filipinos and Americans should have stood shoulder to shoulder instead of appealing to force for their varying immediate aims. But as Carl Schurz sagely remarked, "The best government will always be unpopular if it is foreign government." [2]

When Storey, Hoar and Schurz opposed the Philippine policy of the administration on the ground that "governments derive their just powers from the consent of the governed" they were entirely logical, for the course of events makes it evident that the Filipinos did not desire American rule; but it was no more flagrant a case than the war of the North on the Confederate States, as the Southern people desired a government of their own with slavery amply protected. Lincoln conducted the war on the ground that a majority of the Southern people were not of the same mind as their leaders, and McKinley, Root and Taft made war on the Philippine insurgents with a similar view.

---

[1] As to this see Blount, American Occupation of the Philippines, 365.
[2] Schurz, Speeches, vi. 175.

Portrait by Philip A. de László.

McKinley was a rare judge of men. When he forced
the resignation of Russell A. Alger as Secretary of War, he
appointed to the position Elihu Root of New York. The
appointment was made during July, 1899, and Root thus
told the story: "Having just finished the labors of the
year and gone to my country home, I was called to the
telephone and told by one speaking for President
McKinley, 'the President directs me to say to you that
he wishes you to take the position of Secretary of War.'
I answered, 'Thank the President for me, but say that it
is quite absurd. I know nothing about war. I know
nothing about the army.' I was told to hold the wire,
and in a moment there came back the reply, 'President
McKinley directs me to say that he is not looking for
anyone who knows anything about the army; he has got
to have a lawyer to direct the government of those Spanish islands and you are the lawyer he wants.' Of course,"
proceeded Root, "I had then, on the instant, to determine what kind of a lawyer I wished to be, and there was
but one answer to make, and so I went to perform a lawyer's duty upon the call of the greatest of all our clients,
the government of our country."

Root described his labor: "It was a fascinating work.
It was the work of applying to some ten millions of people
in Cuba and Porto Rico and the Philippines, the principles of American liberty. They were living under laws
founded upon the customs of their lives, customs drawn
from old Spain and developed in social and industrial
activity quite unlike that of the United States; and the
problem was to apply those principles which are declared
in our constitutions, which embodied the formative idea
of the Declaration of Independence that all men are en-

drafted by Root and with "trifling verbal changes" signed by the President.[1] This is asserted by other writers and so far as I know not contradicted, so it may be recorded as a fact. As the military government was now supreme and it was desirable to avoid any conflict with the Civil Commission, both the general in command and the Commission were directed to report to the Secretary of War. The Commission should at first "devote their attention to the establishment of municipal government, in which the natives of the islands, both in the cities and in the rural communities, shall be afforded the opportunity to manage their own local affairs to the fullest extent of which they are capable, and subject to the least degree of supervision and control, which a careful study of their capacities and observation of the workings of native control show to be consistent with the maintenance of law, order, and loyalty." Next should be the organization of government in the large administrative divisions, the intent being to substitute civil for military control. On September 1, 1900, the legislative authority which had been exercised by the military governor should be transferred to the Civil Commission. "Exercise of this legislative authority," the instructions continued, "will include the making of rules and orders, having the effect of law, for the raising of revenue by taxes, custom duties and imports; the appropriation and expenditure of public funds of the islands; the establishment of an educational system throughout the islands; the establishment of a system to secure an efficient civil service; the organization and establishment of courts; the organization and

---

[1] Military and Colonial Policy, 225.

establishment of municipal and departmental governments, and all other matters of a civil nature. . . . Wher-
ever civil governments are constituted under the directions
of the Commission, such military posts, garrisons and forces
will be continued for the suppression of insurrection and
brigandage and the maintenance of law and order as the
Military Commander shall deem requisite, and the military
forces shall be at all times subject, under his orders, to the
call of the civil authorities for the maintenance of law
and order and the enforcement of their authority."

Natives of the islands should be preferred for the offices
but they must be absolutely and unconditionally loyal
to the United States. The government established is
"not for our satisfaction or for the expression of our theo-
retical views, but for the happiness, peace and prosperity
of the people of the Philippine Islands, and the measures
adopted should be made to conform to their customs,
their habits, and even their prejudices to the fullest extent
consistent with the accomplishment of the indispensable
requisites of just and effective government."

Then followed, substantially, the Bill of Rights of the
American Constitution; but the right to bear arms and
trial by jury were not included in the enumeration of the
safeguards of liberty. Education should be promoted
and extended. This was an easy matter as the desire
for education was almost universal and the wish to learn
English eager. With wisdom the direction to the Commission was: "Instruction should be given in the first
instance in every part of the islands in the language of
the people. In view of the great number of languages
spoken by the different tribes, it is especially important
to the prosperity of the islands that a common medium

of communication may be established, and it is obviously
desirable that this medium should be the English language. Especial attention should be at once given to
affording full opportunity to all of the islands to
acquire the use of the English language." The compre-
hensive instructions ended with: A "high and sacred
obligation rests upon the Government of the United
States to give protection for property and life, civil and
religious freedom and wise, firm and unselfish guidance
in the paths of peace and prosperity to all the people of
the Philippine Islands. I," said the President of the
United States, "charge this Commission to labor for the
full performance of this obligation, which concerns the
honor and conscience of their country, in the firm hope
that through their labors all the inhabitants of the Philippine Islands may come to look back with gratitude to
the day when God gave victory to American arms at
Manila and set their land under the sovereignty and the
protection of the people of the United States." [1]

The way was paved by the introduction of a bill from
the Committee on the Philippines which, although not
enacted, offered a statement from Senator Henry Cabot
Lodge, who was in full sympathy with our possession of
the Philippines. On March 7, 1900, he said: The "President, under the military power, which still controls and
must for some time control the islands, could do all that
this bill provides. . . . We follow the well-settled pre-
cedents of Jefferson and Monroe. . . . We may safely
tread in the footsteps of the author of the Declaration of Independence. He saw no contradiction be-

---

[1] Messages and Papers of the President, Supplement, 139.